THIRD EDITION

MASS COMMUNICATION LAW IN IDAHO

Edited by Rebecca J. Tallent
& Robert J. Taylor

NEW FORUMS

NEW FORUMS PRESS INC.

Published in the United States of America
by New Forums Press, Inc.1018 S. Lewis St.
Stillwater, OK 74074
www.newforums.com

Library of Congress Cataloging-in-Publication Data Pending

This book may be ordered in bulk quantities at discount from New Forums Press, Inc., P.O. Box 876, Stillwater, OK 74076 [Federal I.D. No. 73 1123239]. Printed in the United States of America.

ISBN 10: 1-58107-306-2
ISBN 13: 978-1-58107-306-5

Contents

Foreword

Media law in Idaho is sometimes sticky, but is often clear-cut if one takes the time to look up the law. Unfortunately, too many people do not have the time nor the understanding of where to turn for the information.

That is why this book was re-written. The first book was written in 1986, but the first under this title was published in 1992 by New Forums Press and re-issued under another title in 2003. In all cases, the intent of the authors was and is to help people understand media law in the state. A central location to find out about open meetings, shield law, advertising law, defamation and other media law issues in Idaho.

The First Amendment provides protection through freedom of the press and speech. Idaho's constitution goes one step further by stating (Kristensen, 2004): "[e] very person may freely speak, write and publish on all subjects, being responsible for the abuse of that liberty."

As Debora K. Kristensen said in her 2004 Idaho Law Review article:

> Although Idaho has never been a hotbed of First Amendment jurisprudence, media law in Idaho has slowly developed to recognize and be in conformity with long- established First Amendment principles elsewhere. Indeed, Idaho courts at all levels have been confronted with a number of media-related issues in recent years, including defamation, invasion of privacy, reporter's privilege, cameras in the courtroom, and the contours of First Amendment protections for newsgathering. The mere recognition of these principles by Idaho courts has had the effect of expanding media protections in Idaho.

Each writer in this work speaks in their particular voice, and the reader may notice the citation styles differ between American Psychological Association and the lawyer's preferred Bluebook. This is the various authors' personal preference. However, all the chapters are written in common English so anyone can understand the topics.

Many thanks are given to the individuals who worked diligently on this volume: Professors Shaakirrah Sanders, Katie Blevins, and Justin Barnes, all of the University of Idaho, and Susan Dente Ross of Washington State University. Additional thanks goes to Robert J. Taylor, J.D., of Mountain Home, Idaho, for his legal expertise in editing. Also, the authors appreciate the Idaho Press Club, especially Betsy Z. Russell, for their willingness to review and endorse.

Additional thanks go to the predecessors of this book: in 1986, the work of the Idaho attorneys, journalists, and editors who compiled the *Idaho Media Law Handbook*; Roy Atwood's 1992 revision titled *Mass Communication Law in Idaho*; and the 2003 *In the Public Interest* by Russell A. Joki, which revised Atwood's work.

Since 2003, most of the state's media-related laws have been revised. It is the hope of the authors and editors of this work that journalists, attorneys and citizens can find their answers to Idaho's media law today.

Rebecca J. Tallent, Ed.D.
Moscow, Idaho March, 2017

Reference

Kristensen, D.K. (2004). Media law in Idaho: Where are we? *Idaho Law Review, 40*: 395-757.

From the President of the Idaho Press Club

The Idaho Press Club is pleased to endorse this new edition of *Mass Communication Law in Idaho*, which puts many of the laws that affect the media and communications in Idaho into context with their history and case law as well as current legal requirements. We believe this is a valuable reference book for Idaho journalists, attorneys, law students, public officials and citizens, and would also point anyone interested in access to public records or meetings in Idaho to the openidaho.org website, which includes an online "User's Guide" to Idaho's open meeting and public records laws.

I am frequently asked how to submit a request for public records in Idaho. An agency may ask you to fill out and submit a form (which can help speed up the response), but the basic legal requirements are simple: Just put in writing your request for specific public records, along with your contact information and the date. Here's an example of my typical public records request:

> Under the provisions of the Idaho Public Records Law, Idaho Code 74-101 through 74-126, I hereby request copies of the following public records:
>
> -And then I list the records I want access to here.
>
> Thank you very much for your prompt response to this request.

If the records I am requesting may be voluminous and I could be charged a fee – the first 100 pages and first two hours of labor are free – I request to be notified in advance if there will be a charge. Often, I ask if the records could simply be emailed to me. And it's always a good idea to talk with someone at the agency first to make sure you're sending your request to the right person and have clearly identified the records you're seeking.

This book goes well beyond those basics, delving into libel and defamation law in Idaho, obscenity and indecency, privacy, commercial speech, and Native American press law; we commend it, and very much appreciate this update.

Betsy Z. Russell
President, Idaho Press Club

Chapter 1

Open Records in Idaho

By Rebecca J. Tallent, Ed.D.
Associate Professor of Journalism, University of Idaho

Idaho State Law 74-102. PUBLIC RECORDS -- RIGHT TO EXAMINE. (1) Every person has a right to examine and take a copy of any public record of this state and there is a presumption that all public records in Idaho are open at all reasonable times for inspection except as otherwise expressly provided by statute.

Consider each of the following probable scenarios:

- An Idaho citizen wants to know information about a specific seed crop in the state …
- A resident of Meridian wants to see police records of a case which has been to trial and completed …
- A resident of Benewah County wants to looks at the minutes of a county commission meeting …
- Someone wants to review action by the Idaho State University administration after a new building project was announced.

All of these cases have one thing in common: In each case the requestor can use the Idaho Public Records Act to find the information.

Special thanks to Brian Kane, assistant chief deputy in the Idaho Attorney General's Office, for his kind assistance with this chapter.

But knowledge of and access to the state's Public Records Act (Idaho Code §74: 101-126, 2015) is not always clear for citizens, journalists or government officials. In the Idaho Public Records Law Manual (2015), Atty. Gen. Lawrence Wasden explained the Legislature re-codified the law in 2015 "to provide one place for citizens to find laws relating to government transparency." However, Wasden said although he encourages government agencies in all 44 counties to comply with the Public Records Act, it is incumbent on individuals to challenge the government agency's refusal to provide access to the record (Wasden, 2015).

While many states have enshrined the idea of open access to government documents in state constitutions, the Reporters Committee for Freedom of the Press (RCFP) (2016) said statutes – such as Idaho's — and the common law are more frequently invoked to create a presumption of openness in government records.

In Idaho, anyone can ask for public records. Around the country however, notable exceptions include: people who are not citizens of the state (such as in the Commonwealth of Virginia) or residents of the United States who are incarcerated or are not of legal age. The National Association of Counties (NACo) in 2010 also said some states do not allow individuals or corporations use of public records for commercial, political or litigation purposes. Idaho law does not allow for requests to supplant the discovery process in litigation, or for commercial purposes, especially to develop a mailing or telephone call list for a corporation or organization (Idaho Code §§ 74-115(3) & 74-102, 2015).

History

All 50 states have laws requiring open records (RCFP, 2016). Some states – such as Montana – incorporated an open records provision in their constitution (NACo, 2010), but many more already had some form of open or public records provisions before the federal Freedom of Information Act (FOIA) of 1966 and, more recently, the Electronic Freedom of Information Act of 1996 (RCFP, 2016). The federal provisions only deal with federal records, while the state versions are the legal authority for state and local government level public records inquiries. The first FOIA dealt only with paper products, the 1996 law added electronic information, such as emails, texts and other electronic communications, and as a result, many states have revised their open records acts to reflect the inclusion of electronic data and documents.

The Reporters Committee for Freedom of the Press (2016) states while the U.S. Supreme Court has long recognized the right of access to public documents through the First Amendment; jurisdictions within state agencies determine which freedom of information law actually applies in each case. "State open records laws cover most state agencies. In some states, nongovernmental entities that receive public funds or perform a governmental function also are subject to the disclosure laws," said the RCFP (2016).

Born from a 1984 ruling (*Dalton v. Idaho Dairy Products Com'n*, 107 Idaho 6, 684 P.2d 983, 1984).), in 1989 the Idaho legislature began addressing the need for public records and openness in government (Younger, 2015). Younger (2015) said the Idaho Supreme Court held that public records of a state or local unit of government are open for inspection and copying "absent any statutory closure or provision of confidentiality to the contrary." At the time, Younger (2015) said, exceptions to the 1990 public records law were scattered throughout the Idaho Code with 129 separate exemptions for confidentiality. The specific exceptions in the 1990 law included: documents which would invade a person's privacy; ongoing criminal investigations; records deemed confidential under federal law (such as the Family Education Rights and Privacy Act of 1974); juvenile records; adoption records; personnel and employment files; financial, medical and geographic information; and specific trade secrets. Later, information about many other issues, including motor vehicle accident reports, were added to the exception list. In total, by the 2015 legislative session there were 75 specific exceptions to the Idaho Public Records Act.

The 1990 Idaho law said any person, organization or agency could ask for public records, so long as it was not to compile a telephone or mailing list for commercial purposes, of any state agency, officer, department, division, bureau, commission or board, including those in the legislature or judicial branch, except for the state militia. Also included under the law were local agencies, including "county, city, school district, municipal corporation, district, public health district, political subdivision, or any agency thereof, or any committee of a local agency or any combination thereof."

Although listed as covered by the law, the act states the courts have the authority to adopt rules to "govern the disclosure of records of judicial proceedings." Idaho's Supreme Court has adopted Idaho Court Administrative Rule 32 to govern access to judicial records. This rule covers all court records including records that are not part of case files. Additionally, the court has published a media guide to assist the press in navigating the court system.

Younger (2015) said fees for obtaining records under the 1990 Idaho law, updated in 2011, were limited to the actual cost of reproducing the materials, unless the request fell into one of three areas and the agency would include personnel costs into the fee:

- The request for paper records exceeded 100 pages,
- The request required the custodian to segregate nonpublic information from the public portion of the records, and/or
- The labor associated with searching for and copying records exceeded two hours.

Fees could be waived if the individual requesting the records was unable to pay or if "the collection of fees would harm the public's interest." Failure of an agency to provide the requested documents could cost the agency up to $1,000 in fines.

By 2015, Atty. Gen. Lawrence Wasden said there should be one place for the public to find laws concerning government transparency, so the Idaho Public Records Act, along with the Idaho Open Meetings Law, the Ethics in Government Act and the Prohibitions Against Contracts with Officers Chapter were re-codified under Title 74, Transparent and Ethical Government. For the first time in Idaho history, open government and ethics were provided with distinct chapters in their own distinct title making these provisions instantly more accessible to citizens.

The 2015 Idaho Law

Younger (2015), who is the state's Public Records ombudsman, said in early 2014 Gov. C.L. 'Butch" Otter recognized a major flaw in the Public Records Act:

under the law, if a request for records was denied, the only remedy for the requestor was to sue the agency. "The requestor must then take the chance that certain records actually exist and that they do not fall under the exemption cited by the agency," Younger (2015) said. She added the actual cost and risk often outweighed the necessity of the records and acted as a bar to the public, creating an obstacle to increased government transparency. Determining the issue could not be fixed with an executive order, Younger (2015) said Otter turned to the ombudsman to take a broader look at the Idaho Public Records Act.

After a questionnaire was sent to agencies and returned, Younger (2015) said it was clear the act needed modernizing and agencies needed to develop clear policies and fee schedules, and members of the public should be able to make a public records request through an agency's website. During the 2015 legislative session, the Idaho Legislature re-codified the Public Records Law.

In 2016, the Idaho Public Television website's section on public records said the new law now describes "Local agency" as defined in section 74-101(8) includes "a county, city, school district, municipal corporation, district, public health district, political subdivision, or any agency thereof, or any committee of a local agency, or any combination thereof." In the law, "state agency," defined in section 74-101(15), includes "every state officer, department, division, bureau, commission and board or any committee of a state agency including those in the legislative or judicial branch, except the state militia and the Idaho state historical society library and archives."

Idaho Code § 74-102 allows every person the right to examine and take a copy of any public record and requires all public records in Idaho to be open to public inspection. Public records includes any writing containing information relating to the conduct or administration of the public's business. This includes documents which are written (handwritten as well as typewritten, maps, pictures, tapes, magnetic or punched cards and computer media) (Idaho Code §74-101(13)). Although e-mail and texts have not been separately addressed by the legislature, if those messages contain content related to the conduct or administration of the public's business, then they are considered public records (IPRLM, 2015. *Cowles Publishing Co. v. Kootenai County Board of County Commissioners*, 144 Idaho 259, 159 P.3d 896 (2007)).

Under the law, all public agencies – including state, county and local governments, school districts, commissions, political subdivisions, boards, bureaus and divisions, the Office of the Governor, legislature and the judiciary – must maintain records which are available to public access and copying during normal business hours unless those records are exempt (see exceptions below).

Requesting parties do not need to be citizens of Idaho to make a public records request, but an agency may require that all requests must be submitted in writing (Idaho Code § 74-102(4)). Included in the requesting document must be the requestor's name, mailing address, email address and telephone number. Public records requests in Idaho may be submitted via e-mail, and one can request delivery by e-mail as well.

It is recommended that a public records request be as narrowly defined as possible. Broad requests are likely to incur substantial fees. To avoid this scenario, government agencies may provide the requestor information to help them either narrow the request or be more specific when the query is likely to be voluminous (IPRLM, 2015). In sum, an agency may ask a requestor what specifically he or she is seeking, but cannot ask "why?"

Once a request is made, an agency must respond within three days either providing the records or denying the request and identifying the specific exemption claimed for the denial. An agency may take 10 days from the request to locate documents or to redact exempt information from public records. This 10 days should be claimed by the agency with a letter to the requestor explaining the delay. Enforcement of the public records law through a judicial complaint must occur within 180 days of a denial of a public records request.

Although fees can be charged for documents, agencies are prohibited from exceeding the actual cost of copying the paper documents. Electronic documents may also have a charge or fee, but agencies are allowed to charge "the standard cost, if any, for selling the information in the form of a publication" (Idaho Code §74-102 (10) (d)(ii), 2015). The Office of the Attorney General has decided this language permits any agency to charge the cost of the publication if the material requested is already in a printed publication. The law does not stop agencies from recovering mailing or telecommunications costs to deliver the documents.

Labor costs can be recovered under the 2015 law (Idaho Code §74-102(10), 2015) if the agency needs to incur the additional expense of an employee working after hours (including overtime) needs to hire an outside company to assist with copying, or the request exceeds 100 copies and two hours of agency labor. Agencies are allowed to require advance payment for the provision of public records. Such requests for advance payment should include an itemized accounting showing the per page cost, the hourly rates of the employees and attorneys involved in responding and the actual time spent responding to the request. .

Finally, copying fees may be waived if someone cannot afford to pay for the records and/or if the information is sought in a case where the requestor is either already a party to a lawsuit or may become a party, and if the information is "likely to contribute significantly to the public's understanding of the operations or activities of the government." Generally for a waiver, a requestor must demonstrate both an inability to pay and that the request will contribute significantly to the public's understanding of the operations of government (Idaho Code §74-102(10) (f)).

Although the courts have instructed state agencies to construe exceptions narrowly to favor maximum disclosure (NACo, 2010), the state of Idaho specifically exempted the records of the state militia and the Idaho State Historical Society Library and Archives (Idaho Code §74-101 (15), 2015).

Exceptions

While it declares documents and records in the state of Idaho are public, the 2015 law does still contain 99 specific exceptions for areas (up from 75 exceptions in the original law) including: personnel and personal issues (33 exceptions); trade secrets (28 specific exceptions); law enforcement at the courts (16 exceptions); air quality and hazardous waste; draft legislation; archaeological sites; endangered species; libraries and licensing exams; and the Uniform Securities Act. These exceptions, as stated in the law, are:

General exceptions (74-104):

Any public record exempt from disclosure by federal or state law or federal regulations to the extent specifically provided for by such law or regulation.

Records contained in court files of judicial proceedings, the disclosure of which is prohibited by or under rules adopted by the Idaho Supreme Court, but only to the extent that confidentiality is provided under such rules, and any drafts or other working memoranda related to judicial decision-making, provided the provisions of this subsection making records exempt from disclosure shall not apply to the extent that such records or information contained in those records are necessary for a background check on an individual that is required by federal law regulating the sale of firearms, guns or ammunition.

Law Enforcement Exceptions (74-105):

As a general rule, the documents of ongoing investigations are not available under the law. Also exempt from the public are juvenile records for children ages 13 years old and younger (although available to courts, government and private institutions with legitimate concerns, school districts, and private agencies and institutions conducting pertinent research); and review board records for the Idaho Department of Juvenile Corrections (including names, addresses and written statements of victims).

Some records of incarcerated inmates are not public under section 75-105(4) of the Idaho Code, including any information which could lead to the identification of victims or witnesses; information about the future transfer of a prisoner, records gathered during an investigation for presentence determination; records of buildings, infrastructure, facilities and systems which could jeopardize public safety or the safety of prisoners; records of the pardon and parole board and voting records of the sexual offender classification board.

Other exceptions for law enforcement include applicant and licensing records of the sheriff or Idaho State Police; investigation records compiled by the Department of Health and Welfare when dealing with the protection of children, the rehabilitation of youth, adoptions and the commitment of mentally ill persons; information obtained by the manager of the Idaho State Insurance Fund and worker's compensation records obtained by the Idaho State Insurance Fund; records about vulnerable adults compiled by the Commission on Aging; employment, termination of employment, contract or other insurance business relationship between an insurer and producer; compensation for crime victims; and records of a prisoner or former prisoner by another prisoner.

Investigatory records by the Idaho Human Rights Commission are a non-public, unless the public interest outweighs the legitimate public or private interest in maintaining confidentiality. The law further states:

> A person may inspect and copy documents from an investigative file to which he or she is a named party if such documents are not otherwise prohibited from disclosure by federal law or regulation or state law. The confidentiality of this subsection will no longer apply to any record used in any judicial proceeding brought by a named party to the complaint or investigation, or by the Idaho human rights commission, relating to the complaint of discrimination.

Personnel and personal records (74-106)

The largest number of exceptions to the Idaho Public Records Act falls in this category with 33 specific exceptions to the law. The first three deal with protecting employee information of state workers and retired state workers. The rest exempt:

Records considered to be of a "personal nature" such as information provided to public bodies involving personal debt, bank records, ownership of financial obligations (including bonds); securities interests; vital statistics; military records; information concerning income tax or other tax returns measures through sales; applications for public care of the elderly, indigent, mentally or physically disabled; and employment security information.

Other exemptions in this category include: Personal information submitted for bonding; a person's fitness in an application for a license, certificate, privilege, commission or position; private association peer review committee recommendations; pre-litigation screening panels reports; complaints to the board of medicine; recommendations to the Department of Health and Welfare or a health district about a person with a reportable disease; records of hospital care; medical and psychiatric reports that identify a specific patient; information collected for new hired; motor vehicle and driver's license records; the financial state of prisoners; DNA databases and databanks used by the state Police or Department of Corrections; health and welfare records of licensed nursing home investigations (open after investigation is complete, but cannot identify any individual residents); and immunization records.

Still more include: Child support cases from the Department of Health and Welfare; records of the Idaho State Bar Association; records of the trauma registry; court files for sterilization procedures; physical voter registration cards (redacted card copies are OK); file numbers, passwords and information in files of the Health Care Directive Registry (in the Secretary of State's office); records of address confirmation (police and direct court order can override the exception); Idaho Fish and Game license information; documents and records maintained by the Idaho Board of Veterinary Medicine; home addresses and phone numbers of police officers; information between the Idaho Department of Transportation and insurance companies; and information from the administrator of unclaimed property.

Finally the Idaho Housing and Finance Association has several exceptions, including:

- Records containing personal financial, family, health or similar personal information submitted to or otherwise obtained by the IHFA;
- Records submitted to or otherwise obtained by the IHFA with regard to obtaining and servicing mortgage loans and all records relating to the review, approval or rejection by the IHFA of said loans;
- Mortgage portfolio loan documents; and
- Records of a current or former employee other than the employee's duration of employment with the association, position held and location of employment. This exemption from disclosure does not include the contracts of employment or any remuneration, including reimbursement of expenses, of the executive director, executive officers or commissioners of the association. All other personnel information relating to an association employee or applicant including, but not limited to, information regarding sex, race, marital status, birth date, home address and telephone number, applications, testing and scoring materials, grievances, correspondence, retirement plan information and performance evaluations, shall not be disclosed to the public without the employee's

or applicant's written consent. An employee or authorized representative may inspect and copy that employee's personnel records, except for material used to screen and test for employment or material not subject to disclosure elsewhere in the Idaho Public Records Act.

Trade secrets, production records, appraisals, bids, proprietary information (74-107)

Another area with multiple exceptions to the state's Public Records Act, trade secrets are defined by the law as a formula, pattern, compilation, program, computer program, device, method, technique, process, or unpublished or in progress research that:

- Derives independent economic value, actual or potential, from not being generally known to, and not being readily ascertainable by proper means by other persons who can obtain economic value from its disclosure or use; and
- Is the subject of efforts that are reasonable under the circumstances to maintain its secrecy.

Additional exemptions within this section include: Production records, housing production, rental and financing records, sale or purchase of records, catch records, mortgage portfolio loan documents or similar business records of private companies or organizations; records relating to the appraisal of real property, timber or mineral rights; any estimate prepared by a public agency or independent public body that details the cost of a public project until bids are opened; examination, operating or condition reports and all related documents relating to financial institutions; records gathered by a local company for the purposes of investments or business expansion; shipping and marketing records of commodity commissions used to evaluate marketing and advertising strategies and the names and addresses of growers and shippers; and financial statements and business information and reports submitted by a legal entity in a port district organized under Title 70, Idaho Code, in connection with a business agreement.

Specific agricultural exceptions include: Names and addresses of seed companies, seed crop growers, seed crop consignees, locations of seed crop fields, variety name and acreage by variety; information obtained from books, records and accounts under Chapter 47, Title 22 of the Idaho Code maintained by the Idaho Oilseed Commission; active investigative records and trademark use audits of the Idaho Potato Commission relating to the enforcement of formal proceedings; all records copied or obtained by the director of the Department of Agriculture as a result of an inspection, except documents deemed to otherwise be public records not exempt from disclosure and inspection reports, determinations of compliance or noncompliance and all records created by the director under Idaho Code 25-3806; all data and information collected by the division of animal industries or the state brand board; records of laboratory test results provided by the Idaho Food Quality Assurance Laboratory; results of laboratory tests which have no known adverse impacts to human health conducted by the Idaho Department of Agriculture animal health laboratory, related to the diagnosis of animal disease, unless the results indicate the presence of a state or federally reportable disease, the release of test results is required by state or federal law or the results represent a threat to animal or human health or to the livestock industry; and laboratory test results conducted by the Idaho Department of Agriculture on samples submitted by seed producers or seed companies.

Exceptions for academic work include: Records, data, information and materials collected, developed, generated, ascertained or discovered during the course of academic research if disclosure would reasonably affect the conduct or outcome of the research, or if disclosure would impact the higher education institution's ability to achieve copyright or patent or protect the intellectual property; records, data, information and materials collected during academic research which was provided by any person or entity other than the public institution of higher education or a public agency; once academic research is completed, the data should be public unless another exception in the law applies, such information was provided under a written agreement of confidentiality or public disclosure would pose a danger to persons or property, although basic information not otherwise exempted – such as the name of the researcher, the nature of the research and who provided the funding – should be public. Individual financial statements for postsecondary education institutions are also exempt under Sections 33-2404 or 33-2403, Idaho Code.

Under exemptions for taxation, records of a county assessor, the state tax commission, a county board of equalization or the state board of tax appeals which contain lists of personal property, operating statements, confidential commercial or financial information are also exempt, with specific allowances for examination of the records by relevant officers of the state or United States. Also exempt are publication of statistics or reports as long as individuals are not identified, the board of appeals or the district court in the case of an appeal. However, names and mailing address of a property owner, the legal description of real property, the square footage and/or acreage of a property, the assessed value of a taxable property, the tax district rate and the total property tax assessed are public documents.

Other exemptions are: Records of any risk retention or self-insurance program prepared in anticipation of litigation or for analysis of settlement against a public entity (the claims can be public after settlement); reports filed under Chapter 13, Title 62, Idaho Code, identifying electrical or natural or manufactured gas consumption data for an individual customer or account; and voluntarily prepared environmental audits and voluntary disclosure of information submitted on or before December 31, 1997, to an environmental agency that are claimed to be confidential business information.

Records of policies that are owned by private persons including records of endorsements, affidavits and any records that discuss policies, endorsements and affidavits that may be required to be filed with or by a surplus line association under Chapter 12, Title 41, Idaho Code.

Archaeological sites, endangered species, libraries and licensing exams (74-108)

In order to protect archaeological sites which are still under investigation, records, maps or other records identifying the location of an archaeological or geographical site or endangered species not already known to the public are exempt from the Public Records Act.

Also included in this section of the law are: Archaeological and geologic records dealing with the drilling, mining, logging and other excavations; records of a library which might identify a specific patron checking out, using or requesting items from a library; the material of a library, museum or archive that has been contributed by a private person if a limitation has been placed by the contributor; test questions, scoring keys and other data used to administer a licensing exam, employment, academic or other examination or testing before the exam is given; and land management plans required for voluntary stewardship agreements for all species of sage grouse when the landowners or occupiers of land have entered into an agreement with the Soil Conservation Commission.

Draft legislation and supporting materials, Tax Commission, Unclaimed Property, Petroleum Clean Water Trust Fund (74-109)

Legislation can go through many changes prior to submission for consideration, and these are in addition to the many changes that can happen in committee, on the floor and in conference. Therefore, draft legislation and documents specifically related to the drafts are exempt from the Public Records Act until the legislation is introduced. Once it is printed, the legislation is made readily available on the Idaho Legislature's website. Unless otherwise confidential or exempt from disclosure, after the legislation is complete (passed into law or defeated), all papers and records, including correspondence and other supporting documents, will become public once the final fate of the legislation is determined.

Unless members of a commission have specifically waived the right, records detailing draft congressional and legislative redistricting plans remain non-public as do records identifying the method by which the Idaho State Tax Commission selects tax returns for audit review. Similarly, records which identify the method by which the administrator of the unclaimed property law set forth in Chapter 5, Title 14, Idaho Code, selects reports for audit review or conducts audit review of such reports and the identity of individuals or entities under audit.

Underwriting and claims records of the Idaho Petroleum Clean Water Trust Fund obtained pursuant to section 41-4905, 41-4909, 41-4911A, 41-4912 or 41-4912A, Idaho Code are exempt; however, information about corrective action should be disclosed, especially if products are released into the environment from a petroleum storage tank.

Court records authorizing abortion procedures for minors (74-110)

In accordance with section 18-609A, Idaho Code, the following records are exempt from public disclosure: all records contained in court files of judicial proceedings arising under section 18-609A, Idaho Code, are exempt from disclosure.

Records relating to the Uniform Securities Act (74-111)

The following records are exempt from the Public Records Act, unless otherwise determined by the director of the Department of Finance under section 30-14-607(c):

A record obtained or created by the director of the Department of Finance or a representative of the director in connection with an audit or inspection under Section 30-14-411(d), Idaho Code, or an investigation under Section 30-14-602, Idaho Code; a part of a record filed in connection with a registration statement under Section 30-14-301, Idaho Code, and Sections 30-14-303 through 30-14-305, Idaho Code, or a record under

Section 30-14-411(d), Idaho Code, that contains trade secrets or confidential information if the person filing the registration statement or report has asserted a claim of confidentiality or privilege that is authorized by law; and record that is not required to be provided to the director of the Department of Finance or filed under Chapter 14, Title 30, Idaho Code, and is provided to the director only on the condition that the record will not be subject to public examination or disclosure.

Also, a nonpublic record received from a person specified in Section 30-14-608(a), Idaho Code; and any Social Security number, residential address unless used as a business address, and residential telephone number unless used as a business telephone number, contained in a record that is filed pursuant to Chapter 14, Title 30, Idaho Code.

Records relating to confidentiality (74-124)

Some records have been determined by the legislature to be kept confidential and exempt from the Idaho Public Records Act, so no part of these exemptions should be considered to be public.

Specifically, the law states the following are <u>not</u> public records.

Law enforcement

For this section of the law, "law enforcement agency" means the Office of the Attorney General, the Office of the State Controller, the Idaho State Police, the office of any prosecuting attorney, sheriff or municipal police department.

Any record compiled for law enforcement purposes are exempt from disclosure to the extent that the production of such records would interfere with enforcement proceedings; deprive a person of a right to a fair trial or an impartial adjudication; constitute an unwarranted invasion of personal privacy; disclose the identity of a confidential source and, in the case of a record compiled by a criminal law enforcement agency in the course of a criminal investigation, confidential information furnished only by the confidential source; disclose investigative techniques and procedures; or endanger the life or physical safety of law enforcement personnel.

If a person is involved in a motor vehicle accident which is under investigation by law enforcement personnel, that individual's legal representative or insurance provider shall have a right to a complete, unaltered copy of the impact report, or its successors, and a complete final report prepared by the agency.

Inactive investigations under 74-124 (3) may provide specific information, including the time, date, location, nature and description of a reported crime, incident or accident; the name, age, gender and address of the person arrested, except as otherwise provided by law; the time, date and location of the incident and arrest; the crime charged; the documents given to the person arrested; information and indictments, except as otherwise provided by law, and criminal history reports.

The exception section does say if investigative reports are improperly being withheld, the court will order the person withholding the records to disclose the information or show cause why it should not be done. The court will then decide if the materials should be made public or not. If the court decided the withholding of the records is not justified, the record must be made public; but if withholding the documents is justified, the documents will be returned to the public official without the court disclosing the information with an order supporting the refusal for disclosure.

Access to air quality, water quality, and hazardous waste (74-114)

Under federal law, information concerning the Clean Air Act and the Resource Conservation and Recovery Act are open records, so any person may obtain information about air pollution emission data, the content of any Title V operating permit, the name and address of any applicant or permittee for hazardous waste treatment, storage or disposal facility, and under Idaho law, requestors may ask to see any other record to be provided by the Department of Environmental Quality under the federal Clean Air Act and the Resource Conservation and Recovery Act.

What is exempt under state law are the following:

If the information is considered a "trade secret" within the meaning of the Idaho Trade Secrets Act, Section 48-801, et. seq., Idaho Code, including commercial or financial information which may cause competitive harm to the person from whom the record was obtained; if the record is a trade secret, no part of the record will be public.

A continuing confidentiality claim can protect any officer, employee or authorized representative of the state or the United States to carry out the provisions of the state or federal law; the confidentiality claim can also be used to protect the public health and safety from "imminent and substantial endangerment."

It is incumbent on the person or entity claiming the information is a trade secret to give notice of the existence of such trade secret on each page at the time of submission of the information, plus they will have the burden of proof the information is a trade secret. If a request is made for the information and the person or entity has not proven it is a trade secret within three working days of the request, the director of the Department of Environmental Quality will provide a written request for substantiation of the claim with a response due in 10 working days. On receipt of the response, the director decides if the information does meet the standard of trade secret within three working days. If the "trade secret" justification is denied, the director will contact the person making the request to inform them the request was denied under Sections 74-103 (3) and (4), Idaho Code. The person or company requesting the trade secret status can appeal the denial with a written notice; but no disclosure of the information can be made until all appeals have been exhausted.

The Public Records Act requires the Department of Environmental Quality to adopt rules which include appropriate measures to safeguard and protect against improper disclosure of trade secrets, including procedures to train all employees on the proper handling of trade secrets and any other provisions necessary to carry out the section.

Under the section, no agents, contractors or other representatives of the Department of Environmental Quality can apply for the immunity from the Public Records Act unless there is a trade secret clause in effect.

Separation of exempt and non-exempt records

Title 74-112, Idaho Code, requires agencies to separate exempt and non-exempt records when a request is made for the documents. In doing so, the section obliges agencies to have the nonexempt material available for public inspection "and shall not be based upon the fact that such nonexempt material is contained in the same public record as the exempt material."

Enforcement of the Public Records Act

Under the Idaho Public Records Act, citizens can enforce the provisions of the act by filing a complaint within the district court where the records or some portion of the records are located. The agency will then submit the records along with its justification for claiming an exemption from disclosure to the court for review. The court will review the documents and justifications and issue a decision regarding the records. If the court finds an agency has withheld public records in bad faith, the agency may be subject to attorney fees and an additional fine of up to $1,000. The act also provides immunity for public employees who in attempting to comply with the Act inadvertently disclose an otherwise exempt document (Idaho Code § 74-118).

Conclusions

As does many states, Idaho has expressed into law the idea that government is the people's business and, as such, should be open for the citizens to see/inspect/copy its records for their own purposes. However, with the current list of exceptions, the law can seem more of a stop light to documents and information than a green-light. The Reporters Committee for Freedom of the Press (2016) lists Idaho as having one of the largest exceptions list to open records in the country. Idaho is one of the few states which strictly prohibits release of vital statistics and driver's license information in its Public Records Act. While it is commendable the legislature placed all the exceptions under the Public Records Act for easier reference, it is still a lengthy list of exceptions to government records.

Anyone who wants or needs government documents should be aware of the exceptions, and any additional exceptions after each legislative session. Watchdog groups should also keep aware of potential additions to the exceptions.

In the meantime, seekers looking to open records should continue making their requests while being mindful of the exceptions.

A copy of the complete law, Idaho Code § 74:101-126, can be found in Appendix A.

References

Idaho Code § 74:101-126 (2015) Retrieved on Jan. 26, 2016 from the Idaho Legislature website at https://legislature.idaho.gov/idstat/Title74/T74CH1.htm

National Association of Counties (2010, December). Open records laws: a state by state report. Retrieved Jan. 26, 2016 from NASCo website at http://www.naco.org/sites/default/files/documents/Open%20Records%20Laws%20A%20State%20by%20State%20Report.pdf

Open Idaho (2016). "Frequently asked questions about public records." Idaho Public Television website. Retrieved on Jan. 26, 2016 from http://idahoptv.org/dialogue/openidaho/recordsfaq.cfm

Reporter's Committee for Freedom of the Press (RCFP). (2016). "Open government guide."Retrieved on Jan. 26, 2016 from RCFP website at http://www.rcfp.org/open-government-guide

Wasden, L. (2015) Idaho Public Records Law Manual. Retrieved on Feb. 1, 2016 from Idaho Attorney General's Office website at http://www.ag.idaho.gov/publications/legalManuals/PublicRecordsLaw.pdf

Younger, C. (2015, February). "In year 25, Idaho's Public Records law gets a checkup by Idaho's Public records Ombudsman." The Advocate 58 (2) 32-34.

Chapter 2

Idaho Open Meetings Law

By Rebecca Tallent, Ed.D.
Associate Professor of Journalism, University of Idaho

" ... all meetings of a governing body of a public agency shall be open to the public and all persons shall be permitted to attend any meeting except as otherwise provided by this act. No decision at a meeting of a governing body of a public agency shall be made by secret ballot." Idaho Code 74-203.

Idaho's Open Meetings Act has never had an easy life. Originally enacted in 1961, the law has been rewritten twice with multiple amendments and it has been impacted by several court rulings. Kane (2007) described the Idaho Open Meetings Act as a "quilt," between the history and the actual words, the description fits.

It could be considered a lot of trauma for a law to allow people to attend meetings of state, county and city governments.

Much of the trauma came through misinterpretation of the then-laws, other times there was a lack of understanding of terms used – including the term "knowingly" in the 1974 law – and exactly what constitutes a written

---

Special thanks to Brian Kane, assistant chief deputy in the Idaho Attorney General's Office, for his kind assistance with this chapter.

record of a meeting (Kane, 2007); still, the main purpose of the law has consistently been clear: for the business of government to be open (Kane, 2007). The best lens to view the Open Meetings Act through is as a ticket to the show of government. It guarantees government, citizens and the media the ability to observe but not necessarily participate in the meetings of government.

In general, open meetings laws require government agencies – federal, state, county and local – to provide advance notice of a meeting plus the information to be discussed in the meeting through a posted agenda (RCFP, n.d.). The federal counterpart is the Government in the Sunshine Act, which is modeled after the Freedom of Information Act (FOIA) and codified at 5 U.S.C. §§ 1 et seq. As state law stands in 2016, Idaho Code 74-201-203 requires any governing body to conduct all business in open meetings, with 10 exceptions (see below). Idaho's legislature has similarly bound itself to conduct its business in the open through adherence to Article III, § 12 (Secret Sessions Prohibited); and legislative rules limiting the use of executive sessions to specific instances. The Idaho Open Meetings law unequivocally pronounces "it is the policy of this state that the formation of public policy is public business and shall not be conducted in secret (Idaho Code 74-201)." The law defines "governing body" to be members of any public agency "which consists of two or more members, with the authority to make decisions for or recommendations to a public agency regarding any matter" (Idaho Code 74-202).

Definitions included in the law are (Idaho Code 74-202):

- "Decision," means any determination, action, vote or final disposition upon a motion, proposal, resolution, order, ordinance or measure on which a vote of a governing body is required, at any meeting at which a quorum is present, but shall not include those ministerial or administrative actions necessary to carry out a decision previously adopted in a meeting held in compliance with this chapter;

- "Deliberation" means the receipt or exchange of information or opinion relating to a decision, but shall not include informal or impromptu discussions of a general nature which do not specifically relate to a matter then pending before the public agency for decision;
- "Executive session" means any meeting or part of a meeting of a governing body which is closed to any persons for deliberation on certain matters.
- "Public Agency" means
  (a) any state board, commission, department, authority, educational institution or other state agency which is created by or pursuant to statute, other than courts and their agencies and divisions, and the judicial council, and the district magistrates commission;
  (b) any regional board, commission, department or authority created by or pursuant to statute;
  (c) any county, city, school district, special district, or other municipal corporation or political subdivision of the state of Idaho;
  (d) any subagency of a public agency which is created by or pursuant to statute, ordinance, or other legislative act.
- "Meeting" means the convening of a governing body of a public agency to make a decision or to deliberate toward a decision on any matter.
  (a) "regular meeting" means the convening of

a governing body of a public agency on the date fixed by law or rule, to conduct the business of the agency.

(b) "special meeting" is a convening of the governing body of a public agency pursuant to a special call for the conduct of business as specified in the call.

In addition, no public agency is allowed to hold a meeting any place where discrimination exists on the basis of race, creed, color, sex, age or national origin (Idaho Code 74-203(4)).

The law provides for meetings to be held electronically, either as a teleconference or a video conference, as long as one member of the governing body or the executive director are physically located at the location designated by the meeting notice (Idaho Code 74-203(5)).

Prior to all meetings, the law requires a notice to be posted no less than five calendar days prior to the meeting with the meeting agenda posted 48 hours in advance (74-204). Agendas should include all items of probable discussion including items requiring an action of the governing body. Special meetings must post a notice plus the agenda 24 hours in advance, unless an emergency exists.

Executive sessions must be posted on the agenda, stating the specific reason for the executive session and the specific provision of law which would authorize an executive session (74-204(3)). If an agency or public body finds an addition needs to be made to an agenda, the agenda can be amended in one of three ways (Idaho Code 74-204(4)):

- If the amendment is made at least 48 hours in advance of a regular meeting or 24 hours in advance of a special meeting, the amended agenda can be posted in lieu of the original agenda;

- Prior to the start of a meeting (less than 48 hours of a regular meetings and fewer than 24 hours for a special meeting), the proposed amended agenda can be posted, but cannot become effective until a motion is made at the meeting and the governing body votes to amend the agenda.
- An agenda can be amended after the start of a meeting upon a motion that states the reason for the amendment and states the good faith reason the agenda item was not included in the original agenda posting.

All public meetings are required under law to maintain written minutes of meetings and be available for public inspection within a "reasonable time after the meeting" (Idaho Code 74-205) and it should include: names of all members present; all motions, resolutions, orders or ordinances proposed and their dispositions; the results of all votes, and upon request of a member, the vote of each member by name. Minutes, including "draft" minutes are public records and should be made readily available for public review.

Minutes of executive sessions must include a reference to the specific statutory subsection authorizing the executive session and "shall provide sufficient detail to identify the purpose and topic of the executive session but shall not contain information sufficient to compromise the purpose of going into the executive session." (Idaho Code 74-205 (c)).

Executive sessions are limited in scope to only the purpose provided for in the statute, and those purposes are narrowly construed (Idaho Code 74-206(1) & (2). An executive session has specific procedural requirements that must be complied with including a motion indicating the specific provision which the executive session will be conducted, a roll call vote and adoption of the motion by 2/3 of the governing body (74-206(1)).

Similar to other states, Idaho law allows for executive sessions for the purpose of hiring an employee, staff member, public officer or individual agent as well as the evaluation, dismissal, disciplining of or to hear complaints against a public officer, employee, staff member or individual agent. Executive sessions may also be held to acquire interest in real property; consider records which are exempt under the Public Records Act; to consider preliminary negotiations involving trade or commerce in which the state agency is in competition with other states or nations; to communicate with legal staff on pending litigation or controversies "not yet being litigated but imminently likely to be litigated;" and to consider labor contract matters (Idaho Code 74-206).

In addition, executive sessions may be held by the commission on pardons and parole, the custody review board of the Idaho Department of Juvenile Corrections and for agencies to discuss risk management or insurance provider concerning a pending claim or prevention of a claim (Idaho Code 74-206).

The law also comes with a warning for executive sessions (Idaho Code 74-206(2)):

"It shall be a violation of this act to change the subject within the executive session to one not identified within the motion to enter the executive session or to any topic for which an executive session is not provided." Although an agency may be able to enter into an executive session under more than one exception, it cannot change the topic within the executive session to one not permitted under the law within an executive session, or to an otherwise valid executive session topic that has not been noticed on the agenda. Agencies should be vigilant within executive sessions to insure that the discussion does not "drift."

In addition, the law prohibits executive sessions from being used to render any final action or make a final decision. This means that a consensus may be observed within an executive session, but no final action can occur until the governing body returns to an open session. Any action in the open session must be reflected in the minutes.

Idaho Code 74-206A requires agencies to negotiate with labor organizations in open session, although the agency may enter into executive session to discuss the labor contract offer or to receive information about a specific employee which has a bearing on the negotiations "and a reasonable person would conclude that release of the information would violate that employee's right to privacy." All documents exchanged during the negotiations – including all offers, counter offers and meeting minutes – are subject to the public writings disclosure laws; and that public agencies shall post notice of all negotiations "at the earliest possible time practicable."

Violations of the Open Meetings Act can bring the following penalties (Idaho Code 74-208):

Any action or deliberation or decision-making that leads to an action, occurs at any meeting which fails to comply with the act is considered null and void; any member of a governing body who participates in a meeting which violates the law is subject to a penalty not to exceed $250; any member of a governing board who knowingly violates the Open Meetings Act is subject to a $1,500 fine; and any member of a governing body who knowingly violates the act and who previously admitted committing the violation with 12 months of a violation is subject to a $2,500 fine.

Enforcement of the law is directed to the state Attorney General for violations alleged to have been committed by state level and prosecuting attorneys of Idaho's 44 counties for violations alleged to have occurred at the local level. Special prosecutors will be appointed in the event there is reason to believe that a violation has been committed by members of a county commission or if the county prosecutor is disqualified for any reason.

The law offers a remedy for anyone who feels they have been harmed by a violation of the Open Meetings Act, a lawsuit through district court against the offending agency which can only result in an action being declared null and void, no monetary damages can be assessed. Any lawsuit seeking the nullification of a decision needs to be filed within 30 days of the original action, but any lawsuit against an agency not seeking to have the actions declared null and void can be filed within 180 days in a district court.

Agencies have the ability to "cure" a violation of the Open Meetings law. In order to "cure" a violation, the agency has 14 days to respond publically and either acknowledge the error and the intent to cure the violation. If the agency admits there has been a violation, it will have 14 days to take action curing the issue. An agency can also respond to a complaint by indicating that it has not violated the law and there is no need for a cure. Upon that response, any enforcement action may continue as provided for in the court system.

Exceptions

In general, the law states the exceptions for executive sessions must be narrowly construed (Idaho Code 74-206(2)).

There are agencies exempt from the Idaho Open

Meetings Act, specifically: courts and their agencies and divisions, the Judicial Council, the District Magistrates Commission, the Board of Tax Appeals, the Public Utilities Commission and the Industrial Commission (Idaho Code 74-203 (2)), although deliberations of the last three groups may be made in a public setting. Also exempt are the Idaho Life and Health Insurance Quality Association and the Surplus Line Association approved by Idaho Department of Insurance (Idaho Code 74-203 (3)). In addition, the Commission on Pardon and Parole and the Custody Review Board of the Idaho Department of Juvenile Corrections are exempt from the restrictions imposed on all other agencies to hold an executive session (Idaho Code 74-206 (g-h)), expressly allowing these two agencies to hold executive sessions without any specific requirements.

History

As Kane (2007) said, the history of the law is a patchwork. Idaho's Constitution calls for openness in government, specifically calling for the business of the legislature to be conducted in the open and not in secret. It wasn't until 1961 the state enacted an Open Meetings Law; but Kane (2007) said there were significant issues with the law. Of particular concern were areas of vague language, which state agencies interpreted as all meetings outside executive sessions as open, but city and county governments interpreted the law as allowing "unfettered discretion" as to whether a meeting was open or not with the caveat being that no ordinances, resolutions, rules or regulations could be adopted in executive session (Kane, 2007). Likewise, school boards, highway districts and state boards and commission adopted different rules concerning open meetings.

Kane (2007) said the notable missing element was there was no specific rule concerning executive sessions, and no basis on which to base the requirement for such a session. Without procedures and guidelines, various governmental agencies could adopt and follow their own rules.

In 1974 the Idaho legislature amended the Open Meetings Act in an attempt to address the vagaries. House Bill 602 by Rep. Gary Ingram repealed Idaho Code sections 59-1024 and restructured the Open Meetings Law. The new preamble argued the people "do not yield their sovereignty to the agencies so created. Therefore, the legislature finds and declares that it is the policy of this state that the formation of public policy is public business and shall not be conducted in secret" (Idaho Code Ann 67-2340). The 1974 law stated all government meetings are open, prohibited the holding of a meeting where discrimination could occur and – most importantly – required notice of an executive session, including the reason and the specific provision of law for the session (Kane, 2007). The new law also required government entities to keep minutes of their meetings.

But once again there were issues with the law. Specifically there was no penalty clause for any agency breaking the law (Kane, 2007). Four years later, the law was again in the legislature to find a remedy. The legislators did provide financial penalties for agents and officers who unknowingly or knowingly broke the law, but more importantly Kane (2007) said, added language which makes actions of any meetings not in compliance with the law null and void. The same legislative session also added to the list of executive sessions the ability to meet privately with an attorney concerning pending or potential litigation.

The new law was tested in 1981in the case of *State v. City of Hailey*. The county prosecutor alleged the city of Hailey violated the Open Meetings Law when it scheduled four "work sessions" where notice was not given and minutes were not kept (Kane, 2007). The Idaho Supreme Court said the city could be exempt from the law because no firm decisions were reached and people were not excluded.

In 1992 the legislature once again made a significant adjustment to the law when it expanded the scope of the definitions and exempted deliberations of the Public Utilities Commission, the Board of Appeals and the Industrial Commission in certain situations. The 1992 amendments also required the posting of an agenda prior to any meeting and the requirement that public bodies had to give notice if they were only going to meet in executive session. It was in this session the three penalties for knowingly violating the law were also added and people were given the option of a civil lawsuit if they believed the law was violated (Kane, 2007).

Although the legislature did not make any additional changes before 2004, in 2004 the Idaho Press Club sued the legislature for closing several meetings with the use of executive session (Kane, 2007). The Idaho Supreme Court agreed with the legislature, saying the legislature has the constitutional authority under Article III, § 9 of the Idaho Constitution to establish its own rules of proceedings when not acting as a body of the whole or as a specific committee (Kane, 2007).

Even though not Idaho-specific, a Texas case helped to answer an overarching constitutional question in 2011. In *Asgeirsson v. Abbott,* 773 F. Supp. 2d 684 (2011), a

U.S. District Court ruled the Texas Open Meetings Act does not violate the constitutional free speech rights of city officials by requiring them to do business in public (Beckett, 2011). About the case, Beckett (2011) wrote:

> The court found that, contrary to the claims of the plaintiffs, the act does not suppress speech. Rather, the court said that 'free discussion is suppressed when city council members close their meetings to the public.' While council members do have free speech rights, the Open Meetings Act is a disclosure law and is not a content-based restriction on speech, the court held. 'Public officials are allowed to talk about any topic they please; they are only required to disclose what occurred at closed meetings at subsequent open meetings.'

The Yzaguirre Case

Perhaps the most important court challenge to the Idaho Open Meetings Law was what is now known as the Yzaguirre case. In 2005, the Ada County Board of Commissioners (Rick Yzaguirre chair and commissioners Judy Peavey-Derr and Fred Tillman) met in open session on June 15, 2005, and voted to go into executive session with Boise City Councilman Vern Bisterfeldt citing the "litigation exception" of the Open Meetings Law (*State v. Yzaguirre*, 144 Idaho 471, 163 P. 3d 1183, 2007). Votes were not recorded in the handwritten notes of the meeting, but were preserved in an audio recording that was not transcribed, but was available to the public. The executive session was not recorded, nor was the public permitted to attend it. Bisterfeldt later said the group discussed strained city-county relations concerning a potential subdivision approval in the county and the impact of county development on the cost of city services. No pending litigation as discussed, but the commissioners claimed the topics discussed were the subject of litigation in the future. No legal counsel was present for the meeting. The Idaho Supreme Court ruling (2007) explains votes were not recorded in handwritten notes of the meeting, although an audio recording was made, but transcribed, and members of the public were not allowed into the meeting. The Ada County Prosecutor's Office took up the case after a complaint from a private citizen (Kane, 2007).

In the ruling, the Idaho Supreme Court (2007) acknowledged that between the time the case was filed and the issuance of court decision, the Open Meetings Law had already been amended to address the scope the "litigation exception," which made that portion of the case "valueless" (*State v. Yzaguirre*, 2007; Kane, 2007). Although an attorney was not present during the executive session, the court said there was only one possible "grammatically acceptable interpretation" of the now-defunct language (*State v. Yzaguirre*, 2007), and that was an executive session could be held "where there is a general public awareness of possible litigation regardless of the presence of legal counsel (Kane, 2007)."

However, the court did hold the Open Meetings Law was violated because there were no written minutes of the meeting (*State v. Yzaguirre*, 2007). Although the commissioners argued the handwritten notes and audio recording could suffice, the court held that the state specifically requires written minutes. In addition, the court said, the existing handwritten minutes did not clearly state who voted to go into the executive session (*State v. Yzaguirre*, 2007).

A key element of the Yzaguirre case was interpretation of the word "knowing" from the law. Kane (2007) said the state was in a difficult position because the lawsuit said the commissioners were in knowing violation of the law while the commissioners said they thought they were in compliance. The court remanded the question back to the district court (*State v. Yzaguirre*, 2007), but as Kane (2007) said:

> Significantly, the court called the 'knowing' requirement a 'good faith' exception to the civil penalty. But then the court stated the civil penalty is conditioned on the commissioners' mental state. Attorneys and government officials are left to discern what the exact parameters of 'knowingly' and 'good faith' mean.

Solutions

Dealing with the Open Meetings law can be simplified. First, agencies should begin by recognizing that they must comply with the Open Meeting law. Exceptions to compliance are specific and narrow. This means that an agency not having to comply will the exception as opposed to the rule. Executive sessions are permitted under narrow circumstances, but must be entered into from an open meeting in order to comply with the procedural requirements of the law. Every meeting should have a notice and an agenda. Adherence to these requirements establishes a fairly straightforward checklist for compliance. If an agency violates the Open Meetings Law through an oversight, the agency can "cure" that problem through self-recognition, a complaint by a citizen or the press, or through an enforcement action filed in the district court. The law encourages compliance.

There are two parts to the responsibility (Kane, 2010): On the part of agencies, to make sure the law is followed as to openness, posting agendas and keeping minutes of meetings; and citizens need to be alert and notify the local prosecuting attorney if they feel a violation has happened. If a complaint is lodged, agencies need to remember they have 14 days to either acknowledge or deny the law was broken. If the law was violated, the agency must conduct a new meeting which complies with the law. If the agency denies any wrong doing, citizens can file a lawsuit or refer to the prosecutor for further action.

Idaho Attorney General Lawrence Wasden said in the opening to the Open Meetings Act Manual (2015):

> Open and honest government is fundamental to a free society. The Idaho Legislature formalized our state's commitment to open government by enacting the Idaho Open Meeting Law in 1974. The Open Meeting Law codifies a simple, but fundamental, Idaho value: The public's business ought to be done in public

Conclusions

Idaho's promise of open government takes on the appearance of a patchwork quilt when it comes to the Open Meetings Law. While the intent for openness appears to be the history of the law, the vague language and interpretative problems which have plagued it in the past appear to sometimes have erred on the side of secrecy rather than openness.

The segments of the current law addressing executive sessions are set to expire in 2020 (Idaho Code §§ 74-206 & 206A). It is likely that the state legislature will take up these provisions again before that time. Until then, citizens and agencies need to make sure proper agendas are posted and executive sessions are entered into properly so the public's business continues to be conducted in the open.

References

Asgeirsson v. Abbott, 773 F. Supp.2d 684 (2011)

Beckett, C. (2011, March 28). "Court: Meetings act does not violate

First Amendment." Reporter's Committee for Freedom of the Press. Retrieved on June 15, 2016 from RCFP website at http://www.rcfp.org/browse-media-law-resources/news/court-meetings-act-does-not-violate-first-amendment

Idaho Code 74:201-208. (1974). "Title 74, Transparent and ethical government, Chapter 2, Open Meetings Law." Idaho Statutes website, retrieved on March 10, 2016 from https://legislature.idaho.gov/idstat/Title74/T74CH2SECT74-206.htm

Kane, B. (2010, June/July). "A simple premise, a simple process: A practical approach to Idaho's Open Meeting Law." *The Advocate* 22-14

Kane, B. (2007). "Idaho's Open Meetings Act: Government's guarantee of openness or the toothless promise?" *Idaho Law Review* 44 135-169.

Office of the Attorney General (2015). Idaho Open Meetings Law Manual, Idaho Code §§ 74-201 through 74-208. Boise, ID: State of Idaho.

Reporters Committee for Freedom of the Press (n.d.). Digital journalists legal guide: Open meetings. Retrieved from RCFP website on June 14, 2016 from http://www.rcfp.org/browse-media-law-resources/digital-journalists-legal-guide/open-meetings

State v. Yzaguirre, 144 Idaho 471, 163 P.3d 1183 (2007)

Chapter 3

Uncertain Shields

By Susan Dente Ross, Ph.D.
Professor of English, Washington State University

Idaho isn't alone, but it is one of only 10 states that have not passed a state shield law.[1] This doesn't mean journalists who want to protect confidential information and sources from law enforcement officers or courts have no protection whatsoever. It does mean the protection against disclosure is less certain and, usually, more limited than in states with shield laws. It also means journalists cannot legally refuse to disclose nonconfidential information, such as outakes of unpublished information. Newspeople can face fines or jail when they refuse to disclose information sought by government.

Ongoing efforts by the Society of Professional Journalists and other media advocacy groups to push a federal shield law through Congress have been unsuccessful. So reporters who want to protect information and sources from government scrutiny must rely on whatever "reporter's privilege" exists in their state.[2] Each year reporters seem to need this "privilege" more. One recent study found that most newsroom leaders believe government efforts to force reporters to talk are increasing. In a single year journalists received more than 8,000 subpoenas to force their testimony or disclosure of records.[3]

Most journalists agree that shield laws are the best

way to protect journalists from government attempts to jail or even bankrupt reporters as a means to get them to release their information. Like whistleblower statutes, shield laws are intended to protect reporters and their sources from retribution for exposing matters of public importance. As the California Supreme Court noted more than 30 years ago:

> The press function as a vital source of information is weakened whenever the ability of journalists to gather news is impaired. Compelling a reporter to disclose the identity of a source may significantly interfere with this news gathering ability; journalists frequently depend on informants to gather news, and confidentiality is often essential to establishing a relationship with an informant.[4]

Reporters need to maintain their independence, and that of their sources, if they are to function as neutral and objective watchdogs of government and society. Former *New York Times* publisher Arthur Sulzberger once said, journalists:

> enjoy an explicitly defined independence because it is the only condition under which [they] can fulfill [their] role, which is to inform fully, fairly and comprehensively. The crux is not [their] 'freedom to print'; it is rather the citizen's 'right to know.'

Forcing journalists to testify and provide confidential information in court threatens both reporters' credibility with important sources and their access to information vital to the public. Leakers and other sources of information will not feel safe providing the tips, documents and introductions that are the foundation of investigative reporting.

When reporters are forced to disclose confidential

information, people may believe journalists are working *with* government rather than watching over it.[5] Then the watchdog function of the press that is so vital to a functioning democracy breaks down. As the late broadcast newsman Walter Cronkite said:

> A democracy ceases to be a democracy if its citizens do not participate in its governance. To participate intelligently, they must know what their government has done, is doing and plans to do in their name. Whenever any hindrance, no matter what its name, is placed in the way of this information, a democracy is weakened, and its future endangered. This is the meaning of freedom of press. It is not just important to democracy, it is democracy.[6]

Nonetheless, Idaho does not have a state law explicitly setting out rules that protect journalists against subpoenas initiated by prosecutors and law enforcement agencies who want to know what is in their notes, who they spoke with, or what information has been excluded from their published accounts. Instead, journalists working in Idaho may rely only a limited (qualified) privilege that applies only to confidential information and only on a case-by-case basis when the right of the free press is determined to override the right of the public to unfettered law enforcement and legal processes. The Idaho Supreme Court has said, indirectly, that both the federal and the state constitution provide a shield *only* to confidential information.[7]

When you unpack that "privilege," you see that any protection journalists working in Idaho can expect is very tenuous indeed. First, the information must be clearly covered by a promise of confidentiality. Second, the compelled disclosure of that information to government must be seen as a direct infringement on the freedom of the press. Third, the harm caused by the information's forced disclosure must be greater than the harm its withholding would impose on the relevant legal or law enforcement processes.

The determination of each of these three factors is made by the courts based on only a couple of prior court decisions and with the very uncertain guidance of common law. Common law is also "made" by the courts. It is, essentially, the accumulated guidance of decades of court decisions on similar issues.

In *Branzburg v. Hayes*, the U.S. Supreme Court's foundation ruling in this area, the nation's high court in 1972 recognized a qualified reporter's privilege under the First Amendment.[8] In that ruling some 45 years ago, the Court established that the U.S. Constitution affords some protection for newsgathering but not an absolute privilege for reporters to refuse to disclose confidential sources in a criminal investigation. One justice spoke directly to the reason for the limited nature of the reporter's privilege not to testify. He wrote, "We are asked to create ... a testimonial privilege that other citizens do not enjoy. This we decline to do."[9]

In its *Branzburg* decision, the court encouraged states to "fashion their own standards [regarding] relations between law enforcement officials and press."[10] More than a decade later, the Idaho Supreme Court expressly recognized a "substantially similar" limited reporter's testimonial privilege under Article I, Section 9 of the Idaho Constitution.[11] *In the Matter of Contempt of Wright*, also known as *State v. Kiss,* Idaho's highest court found a basis for a qualified reporter's privilege in common law as well. The state's supreme court, however, rejected the existence of any qualified privilege for newspersons to refuse to disclose *nonconfidential* information.

The case arose in 1985 in Moscow, Idaho, when reporter Jim Wright of the *Daily Idahonian* refused to disclose the name of his confidential source for a story about growing marijuana. Wright's testimony was sought to substantiate the claims made by a co-defendant against Gary Kiss, who was on trial for felony manufacture and possession of marijuana. Wright refused to provide the name of his source, a grower, because he had given a promise of confidentiality and believed that promise was vital to the source's willingness to provide information. The trial court found Wright in contempt and levied a fine of $500 per day.

On appeal, the prosecution said Wright's testimony was needed to corroborate the word of Kiss's co-defendant because state law prohibited a conviction based solely on the testimony of an accomplice. In reviewing the appeal, the Idaho Supreme Court reversed the judgment against Wright but refused to establish a broad newsperson's privilege not to disclose confidential information. Instead, it said a limited privilege *may* exist when the press interest in protecting sources as a prerequisite for obtaining information is so paramount that it exceeds the legitimate needs of a criminal plaintiff or the prosecution. "A careful balancing by the courts between a First Amendment privilege, and any interest asserted which may conflict with that privilege, will serve the parties and the public most appropriately," the court said. When the information sought is "so relevant and so material as to be at the very heart" of the legal process, the Idaho Supreme Court said, disclosure may be warranted.

To reach its decision in *The Matter of Contempt of Wright*, the Idaho Supreme Court refused to follow the precedent it had established eight years earlier,[12] when it had held that no reporter's privilege existed in Idaho.

Instead, the justices looked outside of Idaho toward an increasing trend to protect reporters and their sources from government intrusions. Quoting a court in Washington, D.C., the Idaho Supreme Court wrote:

> Without an unfettered press, citizens would be far less able to make informed political, social, and economic choices. . . . Compelling a reporter to disclose the identity of a source may significantly interfere with his news gathering ability; journalists frequently depend on informants to gather news, and confidentiality is often essential to establishing a relationship with an informant.[13]

The court then directed the trial court to review its contempt ruling using the three-part evaluation outlined in *Branzburg.* To determine whether court-ordered disclosure is justified, a court must determine that 1) the journalist is reasonably believed to have the information (There is probable cause.), 2) the information sought is clearly central to the legal proceeding at issue (It lies at the very heart of it.), and 3) alternate sources of the information sought do not exist (and have been explored).

The trial court never held that review hearing. Two years had passed since the court's contempt ruling against Wright, and "nobody cared anymore," he said. "No one ever called for a hearing to decide (if the criteria were met), and the dope in the evidence locker … rotted away."[14]

A decade later, in 1996, an Idaho Supreme Court ruling established one clear exception to the qualified reporter's privilege established by *Wright*. This case did not involve confidential information or sources. Instead it began when Michael Salsbury, a reporter for *The Twin Falls Times-News* was arrested for obstructing and resisting a police officer at the scene of a fatal car crash. The prosecutor sought disclosure of a videotape made at the scene, only portions of which were broadcast by KMVT Broadcasting in Twin Falls.

KMVT challenged the subpoena but provided the tape to the appeals court for *in camera* (closed) review to determine its relevance. The court found the tape showed Salsbury three times, disclosed no confidential information and was made in an area adjacent to a highway that was publicly visible and accessible. The court did not apply the three-part test set out in *Wright*. Instead, it said made clear that the *Branzburg* evaluation used in *Wright* applied only when the information sought was confidential. In this case, disclosure of the tape would expose no confidential information. As a consequence, the court said, its release posed no realistic threat to newsgathering and no infringement on the freedom of the press to disseminate information. Therefore, reporter's privilege did not apply. The court denied KMVT's motion to quash the subpoena.

The Idaho Supreme Court agreed. In its final word on reporter's privilege to date, the court said a newsperson's qualified privilege is limited to situations where journalists want to protect confidential informants or information. There is no privilege for reporters to refuse to disclose nonconfidential information. Even when confidentiality is involved, newspeople can be forced to disclose the information if a court determines that the information is solely in the reporter's possession and is vital to the ongoing case. The court weighs the possible damage of disclosure to the free flow of information to the public against the public's right to have a fully informed court process.

The reporter's freedom hangs in that uncertain balance. If the balance weighs in favor of the courts, refusal to disclose information can land a reporter in jail indefinitely with heavy fines. It can bankrupt a news organization. That can be a very stiff price to pay.

Endnotes

1 The other states without shield laws in 2016 are Iowa, Massachusetts, Mississippi, Missouri, New Hampshire, South Dakota, Vermont, Virginia and Wyoming.

2 *Raise the Shield,* accessed June 3, 2016, at http://www.spj.org/shieldlaw.asp.

3 *Shield Law 101,* accessed June 3, 2016, at http://www.spj.org/shieldlaw-faq.asp.

4 Mitchell v. Superior Court, 690 P.2d 625 (Cal. 1984).

5 *The Reporter's Privilege Compendium,* accessed June 3, 2016, .

6 *Speaking of a Free Press,* accessed June 3, 2016, at http://nieonline.com/thelearningforum/downloads/napi/speaking_of_a_free_press.pdf

7 In the Matter of Contempt of Wright, 700 P.2d 40 (Idaho 1985). *But see* State v. Salsbury, 924 P.2d 208 (Idaho 1996).

8 408 U.S. 665 (1972).

9 408 U.S. at 690.

10 408 U.S. at 706.

11 In the Matter of Contempt of Wright, 700 P.2d 40 (Idaho 1985).

12 Caldero v. Tribune Pub. Co., 562 P.2d 791 (Idaho 1977). *See also* Marks v. Vehlow, 671 P.2d 473 (Idaho 1983).

13 700 P.2d at 42.

14 Spence, William L. "Confidential Sources," Communicator (Summer 2010) accessed June 4, 2016, at http://www.idahopressclub.org/confidential-sources/

Chapter 4

Defamation and Libel

By Shaakirrah R. Sanders
Associate Professor of Law, University of Idaho

Overview

Idaho, like most states, recognizes two types of claims for defamation: libel and slander.[1] Although both represent two distinct categories of defamation,[2] each requires a general showing of damage to one's reputation by the communication of defamatory statements about or concerning the damaged individual.[3] Slander involves unrecorded oral publication of a defamatory statement.[4] Libel involves recorded or written publication of a defamatory statement[5] and includes radio and television broadcasts.[6] Thus in Idaho most defamation cases against the media are claims for libel, not slander.

Idaho Code 18-4801 defines "libel" as follows:

> "a malicious defamation, expressed either by writing, printing, or by sins or pictures, or the like, tending to blacken the memory of one who is dead, or to impeach the honesty, integrity, virtue, or reputation, or publish the natural or alleged defects, of one who is alive, and thereby exposed him to public hatred, contempt or ridicule."[7]

Section 18-4801 is a criminal statute. There is no civil libel statute in Idaho.[8] However, in a 1941 case, *Sweeney v. Capital News Publishing Company*,[9] a federal district court noted that the Idaho Supreme Court applied the criminal statute "to civil actions for libel brought against newspapers and persons."[10]

In 1939 in *O'Malley v. Statesman Printing Company*,[11] the Idaho Supreme Court abandoned the English common law rule that allowed a plaintiff to bring a libel claim against the media in any county of circulation.[12] The *O'Malley* court also acknowledged that the common law rule encouraged or permitted plaintiffs to "select at their pleasure any judicial forum" that would produce a favorable verdict.[13] The court highlighted the inefficiencies and unfairness of the common law rule:

> "It is common knowledge newspapers are widely circulated and read. In the case at bar, copies of the Statesman containing the editorial in question circulated in all the forty-four counties of the state-not less than 7,000 in Ada county and approximately 70 in Bannock. Assuming, but not conceding each copy of the paper circulated would constitute a distinct, separate and independent publication and, therefore, a distinct, separate and independent cause of action, as contended by respondent, our statute would provide forty-four different venues, and as many separate causes of action as there happened to be papers circulated and read in each county-in Ada county alone respondent's causes of action would mount to at least 7,000 as a result of publishing the editorial in a single edition of the paper."[14]

O'Malley ultimately held that Idaho's legislature abrogated the common law rule.[15] Defamation claims must be filed in the county where the cause of action arose.[16] The court declared that in cases against the media, a cause of action in libel arose in the county where publication occurred.[17]

The Idaho Supreme Court often turns to the *Restate-*

ment (Second) of Torts when interpreting state libel law. Section 558 of the *Restatement* identifies four elements of a cause of action for defamation:

> "(1) a false and defamatory statement concerning another;
> (2) an unprivileged publication to a third party;
> (3) fault amounting at least to negligence on the part of the publisher; and
> (4) either actionality of the statement irrespective of special harm or the existence of special harm caused by the publication."[18]

Section 568 of the *Restatement* contains the same distinction between libel and slander that exists in Idaho.[19] Section 568A also makes clear that "[b]roadcasting of defamatory matter by means of radio or television is libel, whether or not it is read from a manuscript,"[20] thus placing broadcasters and publishers on the "same footing."[21] Some states, not Idaho, treat broadcast news as slander rather than libel.[22]

Section 560 of the *Restatement* makes clear that no recovery lies in defamation for the descendants or estate of a deceased person.[23] Section 564A discusses defamation claims concerning a group or class of persons.[24] Sections 561 and 562 provide for causes of action against corporations, partnerships, and associations.[25]

The *Restatement* makes clear that a false or defamatory statement can be a statement of fact or an expression of opinion.[26] Both are actionable if they "tend so to harm the reputation of another as to lower him in the estimation of the community or to deter third persons from associating or dealing with him."[27] Statements of fact can include "accusations of a particular act" or accusations of a particular omission.[28] Expressions of opinion are actionable only where they imply an "allegation of undisclosed defamatory facts as the basis for the opinion."[29] Sections 581A and 583 provide the only two defenses to defamation: truth and consent.[30] Sections 585-612 discuss the absolute and conditional privileges against an action for defamation.[31]

The *Restatement* defines a publication as the intentional or negligent communication of defamatory matter "to one other than the person defamed."[32] The *Restatement* draws a distinction between publication and publicity.[33] Publication is "any communication" by a defendant "to a third party."[34] Publicity involves making the matter "public, by communicating it to the public at large, or to so many persons that the matter must be regarded as substantially certain to become one of public knowledge."[35] According to the *Restatement*, the difference between publicity and publication is not "the means of communication," but whether the communication was private or public.[36] In this sense, any publicity could constitute a publication, but not all publication should be considered publicity.[37] According to the *Restatement*, a single publication occurs when a communication is "heard at the same time by two or more third persons."[38] A separate publication occurs for "each of several communications to a third person by the same defamer."[39] Only one action for damages can be maintained as to any single publication.[40] However, republishers—defined as those who repeat or republish defamatory materials—can be liable as if they were the original publisher.[41]

The *Restatement*'s requirement of proof of damages varies depending on whether the alleged defamation constitutes libel per se.[42] In general, Section 621 allows awards for general damages for a successful claim of libel.[43] General damages are "a form of compensatory damages" and "are imposed for the purpose of compensating the plaintiff for the harm" caused by the publication.[44] Section 569 provides: "One who falsely publishes matter defamatory of another in such a manner as to make the publication a libel is subject to liability to the other although no special harm results from the publication."[45] Special damages are "the loss of something having economic or pecuniary value."[46] Where alleged defamation constitutes libel per se, no proof of special damages is required.[47] Where alleged defamation does not constitute libel per se, special harm may only be recovered where shown.[48]

Idaho also recognizes that defamation claims against the media are limited by the First Amendment.[49] The First Amendment applies a heightened standard of liability referred to as the *New York Times* privilege.[50] The United States Supreme Court first announced this heightened standard in 1964 in *New York Times v. Sullivan*.[51] The *New York Times* privilege requires a plaintiff to prove "actual malice" on certain tort claims against the media.[52] Actual malice requires that the material at issue be published knowing of its falsity or with a reckless disregard for truth.[53] As will be discussed below, subsequent rulings from the United States Supreme Court have expanded the *New York Times* privilege to apply against public officials *and* public figures who bring claims for defamation against the media. Where the alleged defamatory speech is of public concerns, the privilege applies to the recovery of presumed and punitive damages regardless of one's status as a public or private figure or official.

This chapter outlines Idaho libel and defamation cases against the media, with an emphasis on the First Amendment. This chapter begins by presenting the primary Idaho Supreme Court opinions on defamation against the media prior to 1964. Next, this chapter presents *New*

York Times v. Sullivan and its progeny, which impose First Amendment privileges against defamation and libel claims in Idaho. This chapter concludes by presenting the primary Idaho Supreme Court opinions on defamation against the media after 1964.

Idaho Defamation and Libel Cases Against the Media Before *New York Times v. Sullivan*

Idaho's definition of libel dates back over a century. In *Dwyer v. Libert*,[54] a 1917 case, the Idaho Supreme Court defined libel using the exact language of the current statute:

> "a malicious defamation, expressed either by writing, printing, or by signs or pictures, or the like, tending to blacken the memory of one who is dead, or to impeach the honesty, integrity, virtue, or reputation, or publish the natural or alleged defects, of one who is alive, and thereby exposed him to public hatred, contempt or ridicule."[55]

On whether particular words were actionable per se, the court identified a distinction that lies between written and spoken defamation.[56] The court looked to Missouri law and reasoned that "writing or printing injurious statements about a person implies a deliberate purpose to do harm, whereas detrimental words are often spoken thoughtlessly or in a passion."[57] As a result, "[w]eight is allowed . . . to the more enduring character and wider vogue of published statements."[58]

As demonstrated in *Dwyer v. Libert*, prior to 1964 the analysis in Idaho defamation cases against the media primarily involved whether an alleged publication was libelous per se. If a publication was libelous per se, a plaintiff was not required to prove an actual injury. If a publication was not libelous per se, a plaintiff was required to show that damages actually are attributable to that publication. For example in a 1923 case, *Jenness v. Co-operative Publishing Company*,[59] copartners brought a defamation action against the Idaho Free Press, who published the following content:

> "Jenness, Hoy & Co. try to put over big coup. Meeting at City Hall to take fall out of Free Press blows up when aims are revealed. Editorial seized as pretext for joining hands with Capital City interests in an attempt to scuttle Nampa. Jenness of the Leader Herald and the loop reporter of the Capital News, galled by the inroads the Free Press has been making in their business, read the editorial to the languid spectators at Jenness' meeting, and got themselves so stirred up over it that, begorrah, they began to yell for a bomb themselves. They were going to blow up the Free Press building, bedad.
> "Corporation boosters, camouflaged as patriots, with Lanson, Jenness and Hoy at their head * * * the motive being to discipline the Free Press and to acquire for Jenness the authority to write its editorials."[60]

The jury awarded the copartners damages in the amount of $100 and the defendants moved for a new trial on the grounds that the publication was not libelous per se.[61]

The court in *Jenness* explained a key distinction between that which is libelous per se and that which is not. The court expressed disbelief that the Idaho Free Press intended their statements to be taken literally; instead the article sought to adversely direct public opinion by using hyperbole, ribaldry, and caricature.[62] The court described the article as not "a classic in English literature" and snarked that hyperbole, ribaldry, and caricature are useful for writers who lack the "necessary skill or cleverness to express themselves in a more parliamentary manner" of speech.[63] Hyperbole, ribaldry, caricature are not considered to be libel per se because to do so "would result in a vast amount of unimportant litigation."[64] This required Jenness to prove actual damages.[65] Jenness testified at trial that he "knew of no actual loss to [his] business" that resulted from the publication.[66] Instead, his "business had actually grown better, aside from a week or two following" the publication. Thus, Jenness was unable to show damages.[67]

In order to prove libel per se, the publication must have impeached "honesty, integrity, virtue, or reputation" or expose one to "public hatred, contempt or ridicule."[68] In 1952, the Idaho Supreme Court explained in *Gough v. Tribune-Journal Company* (*Gough I*)[69] how to analyze the issue. *Gough I* involved an article published in the Idaho State Journal.[70] The article alleged, among other things, that a commissioner of Bannock County, walked out of a budget meeting in violation of her public duty and in violation of section 18-315 of the Idaho Code.[71] Section 18-315 punished public officers for the willful failure to perform any duty imposed by law.[72] Gough alleged that the article caused damage by injuring her good name and reputation.[73]

The court in *Gough I* looked at the publication at issue from the viewpoint of an ordinary person of average intelligence.[74] A finding of libel per se cannot be based on language that was merely unpleasant, language that annoyed or irked the plaintiff, or language that subjected the plaintiff to "jests or bander."[75] Instead, the "defamatory words must be of such a nature that the court can presume as a matter of law that they will tend to disgrace and degrade the person or hold him up to public hatred, contempt, or ridicule or cause him to be shunned and avoided."[76] Additionally, the words must reflect on an individual's integrity, character, good name and standing in the community or expose an individual to "public hatred, contempt or disgrace."[77]

In 1954, the Idaho Supreme Court decided *Gough v. Tribune-Journal Company* (*Gough II*),[78] which concerned the identical alleged libelous publication as that involved in *Gough I*.[79] There, the court explained that if the language used in a publication "is plain and unambiguous, it is a question of law for the court to determine whether it is libelous per se."[80] Where the plain and unambiguous language used in a publication was not libelous per se, it cannot be made so by innuendo.[81] *Gough II* limits the use of innuendo "where the language of the alleged defamation is so vague or ambiguous" that "explanatory allegations are required to show the intent of the defendant, and the sense in which the article is understood by its readers."[82]

With regards to those in public office, *Gough I* and *Gough II* also demonstrate how Idaho law was already moving in the direction of future United States Supreme Court jurisprudence. *Gough I* held that those in public office, one could not "expect all remarks made concerning them to be complimentary."[83] The court expressed fear that an "unlimited number of suits against newspapers or other publications" would result if a cause of action were allowed for publications that did nothing more than offend a public official's feelings.[84] Moreover, "newspapers would be so bridled as never to know what articles could or could not be safely published."[85] As a result, newspapers in Idaho had the right to make fair comment on acts of public officers and report proceedings and actions taken by elective officers without being subject to damages for libel.[86] *Gough II* explained that publishers in Idaho enjoyed a conditional privilege to critique the public conduct of government officers, employees, municipal corporations, and "all candidates for such office and applications for such employment in so far as the conduct of such officer, employee or candidate is a matter of public concern to those to whom the criticism is published."[87] Where the conditional privilege applied, the publisher was liable only when the exercise of the privilege was abused.[88] Next, this chapter discusses how First Amendment jurisprudence officially altered libel cases against the media in Idaho.

New York Times v. Sullivan and Other First Amendment Limitations on Defamation Claims Against the Media

As mentioned, prior 1964 Idaho law was already moving in the direction of future United States Supreme Court jurisprudence, particularly *New York Times v. Sullivan*[89] which declared that the libel laws of most states were constitutionally deficient.[90] The *New York Times* Court held that a libel action brought by a public official against critics of his official conduct required proof of actual malice.[91] The Court would ultimately extend the *New York Times* privilege to apply against public figures in *Curtis Publishing Company v. Butts.*[92] The Court would later hold in *Gertz v. Robert Welch, Inc.*[93] that *New York Times* privilege also applied to punitive damages in a defamation case that involved the publication of information within the public's interest or concern. However, in *Dun & Bradstreet, Inc. v. Greenmoss Builders, Inc.*,[94] the Court held that the *New York Times* privilege did not apply to punitive damages in a defamation case that involved the publication of private information about a private figure. Finally, the *New York Times* privilege has been extended to claims involving intentional infliction of emotional distress[95] and invasion of privacy.[96]

New York Times v. Sullivan involved a libel claim brought by L.B. Sullivan, who had been elected one of three commissioners for Montgomery, Alabama.[97] Sullivan brought the lawsuit in response to an "editorial" advertisement that the New York Times published on March 29, 1960.[98] The editorial claimed abuse of and sought financial support on behalf of African-Americans who, among other things, sought the right-to-vote in Jim Crow Alabama.[99] None of the statements in the editorial mentioned the name of the commissioners, but Sullivan "contended that the word 'police' in the third paragraph referred to him as the Montgomery Commissioner who supervised the Police Department."[100] Sullivan also "claimed that the paragraph would be read as imputing to the police, and hence to him."[101] Finally, Sullivan contended that since arrests are ordinarily made by the police, statements in the editorial referring to "the 'They' who did the arresting" would be read as referring to Sullivan.[102] Sullivan concluded that the editorial could "be read as accusing the Montgomery police, and hence" Sullivan, of answering civil rights "protests with 'intimidation and violence,' bombing . . . homes, assaulting . . . persons, and charging [Dr. Martin Luther King] with perjury."[103] Sullivan "and six other Montgomery residents testified that they read some or all of the statements as referring to him in his capacity as Commissioner."[104] After a trial, a jury awarded Sullivan $500,000 in damages, which was upheld by the Alabama Supreme Court.[105]

The Court in *New York Times* held that Alabama's libel law—and ultimately the libel laws of most states—was constitutionally deficient for failure to protect freedom of speech and of the press.[106] The Court declared the cause of action for libel "claim[ed] no talismanic immunity from constitutional limitations" and "must be measured by standards that satisfy the First Amendment."[107] The First Amendment protects the "unfettered interchange of ideas for the bringing about of political and social changes desired by the people."[108] A fundamental principle of "our constitutional system" is the "maintenance of the opportunity for free political discussion" as a mechanism to force government response "to the will of the people" in a way that is lawful and "essential to the security of the Republic."[109] The ability to speak one's mind was described as a "prized American privilege" that "presupposes that right conclusions are more likely to be gathered out of a multitude of tongues, than through any kind of authoritative selection."[110]

Turning its attention to Alabama's cause of action for libel, the *New York Times* Court fashioned a new "federal rule" or "privilege" for libel cases against the media.[111] That rule prohibited a "public official from recovering damages for a defamatory falsehood relating to his official conduct unless he proves that the statement was made with 'actual malice'—that is, with knowledge that it was false or with reckless disregard of whether it was false or not."[112] The rule—which has come to be known as the *New York Times* privilege—extends "to a great variety of subjects and includes matters of public concern, public men, and candidates for office."[113] This broad interpretation reflects the First Amendment's "profound national commitment to the principle that debate on public issues should be uninhibited, robust, and wide-open" and that debate on public issues required tolerance of "vehement, caustic, and sometimes unpleasantly sharp attacks on government and public officials."[114] The Court noted that Alabama's libel statute allowed a presumption of malice on the issue of general damages.[115] This presumption was inconsistent with the new federal rule.[116] The Court therefore applied the *New York Times* privilege in all libel actions for damages against public officials.[117]

The question of whether the *New York Times* privilege also applied to public figures, not only public officials, was presented in 1967 in *Curtis Publishing Company v. Butts* and its companion case, *Associated Press v. Walker*.[118] The lead case, *Curtis Publishing Company*, involved a Saturday Evening Post article that accused Wallace Butts "of conspiring to 'fix' a football game between the University of Georgia and the University of Alabama."[119] At the time of publication Butts was the athletic director of the University of Georgia, but he "maintained an interest in coaching and was negotiating for a position with a professional team."[120] Butts resigned from University of Georgia after the article was published, although the stated reasons were for health and business.[121] Butts brought a state libel action in Georgia federal court.[122] A jury awarded Butts $60,000 in general damages and $3 million in punitive damages.[123] The trial court reduced total damages to $460,000.[124] In *Associated Press* a news dispatch reported events on the campus of the University of Mississippi during a time when massive riots occurred over federal enforcement of desegregation decrees.[125] According to an eyewitness, Edwin Walker took "command of the violent crowd and . . . personally led a charge against federal marshals."[126] Walker was a private citizen at the time of the riot and publication, but had previously been in command of federal troops during a school segregation confrontation in Little Rock, Arkansas.[127] The news dispatch concluded that Walker was motivated to incite rioters to violence because of his acute interest "in the issue of physical federal intervention" on the issue of desegregation.[128] Walker brought a libel suit in Texas state court.[129] The jury awarded Walker

$500,000 in compensatory damages and $300,000 in punitive damages.[130] The trial judge rejected the punitive damage award because Walker's evidence of actual malice was insufficient.[131]

The consolidated cases declined to draw a distinction between "public figures" and "public officials" for purposes of the First Amendment.[132] The Court rejected the contention "that criticism of private citizens who seek to lead in the determination of . . . policy will be less important to the public interest than will criticism of government officials."[133] The Court identified the "dissemination of opinion on matters of public interest . . . [as] an 'unalienable right,'" but not an unlimited one.[134] In the same way that a business is not generally immune from regulation, the "publisher of a newspaper has no special immunity" and "no special privilege to invade the rights and liberties of others."[135] However, acceptable limits on the press "must neither affect 'the impartial distribution of news' and ideas . . . nor deprive our free society of the stimulating benefit of varied ideas because their purveyors fear physical or economic retribution solely because of what they choose to think and publish."[136]

The consolidated cases reflected on the evolution and history of libel law, which according to the Court was "entirely different from that which nurtured" U.S. constitutional values.[137] "Early libel was primarily a criminal remedy, the function of which was to make punishable any writing which tended to bring into disrepute the state, established religion, or any individual likely to be provoked to a breach of the peace because of the words."[138] While modern libel law has changed to accommodate the "highly cherished right of free speech," some of its basic theories have not changed.[139] Truth of the underlying facts marks the line between publications with significant social value and publications whose suppression would impose no "serious social harm."[140] However, a finding of falsity alone does not strip constitutional protections.[141]

Because of the similarities between public officials and public figures, state libel actions brought by public figures cannot be left entirely unlimited by constitutional safeguards.[142] While at the time of publication, neither Butts nor Walker were public officials both "commanded a substantial amount of independent public interest" such that they "would have been labeled 'public figures' under ordinary tort rules."[143] Butts attained public figure status "by position alone," while Walker obtained "public figure" status by thrusting himself "into the 'vortex' of an important public controversy."[144] Much like public officials, both Butts and Walker "had sufficient access to the means of counterargument to be able 'to expose through discussion the falsehood and fallacies' of the defamatory statements.'"[145] This similarity between public officials and public figures left the Court convinced that libel actions brought by public figures could not be "unlimited by any overriding constitutional safeguard."[146]

Seven years after *Curtis Publishing Company* and *Associated Press*, the Court was again asked to extend the *New York Times* privilege to cases that involved a matter in the public interest, but did not involve a public official or figure. *Gertz v. Robert Welch, Inc.*[147] involved a publication in the "American Opinion, a monthly outlet for the views of the John Birch Society."[148] In that article, the murder trial of a Chicago policeman was described as "a Communist campaign against the police."[149] The article accused Elmer Gertz, an attorney who had been retained to represent the family of the murder victim, as being involved in the "frame-up."[150] Gertz was also described as having a criminal record and being a "Communistfronter."[151] The jury returned a verdict for Gertz.[152] The federal court trial judge reversed and held the *New York Times* privilege applied to media discussion of a public issue without regard to whether the person defamed is a public official or a public figure.[153] The federal court of appeals agreed.[154]

Gertz affirmed that even after *New York Times* states like Idaho retain "substantial latitude" to determine the extent of a private individual's recovery of general damages in defamation.[155] Private individuals have fewer opportunities for rebuttal than public officials and public figures.[156] Private individuals are also more vulnerable to injury from defamation and thus have an increased risk of injury from defamatory falsehoods.[157] To the extent that private individuals are also more deserving of recovery, the state has a greater interest in compensation.[158] Extending the *New York Times* privilege to private persons would too much abridge that interest. Thus, where the plaintiff is a private figure, actual malice is not required to recover general damages in libel.[159]

Gertz also clarified that the *New York Times* privilege does not apply solely because defamatory statements related to an issue of "public or general interest."[160] The Court ultimately held that Gertz was neither a public official nor a public figure and therefore actual malice was not required for a recovery of general damages.[161] However, the Court made clear that Gertz's recovery may only be had for actual injury.[162] Where the First Amendment applies both presumed damages, which are awarded in cases involving libel per se, and punitive damages require a showing of actual malice.[163]

Dunn & Bradstreet, Inc. v. Greenmoss Builders, Inc.[164] re-examined *Gertz* with regards to the application of the *New York Times* privilege to *presumed* and *punitive damages* in cases brought by a private individual where the alleged defamation did not involve an issue of public concern. Dunn & Bradstreet, a non-media defendant, sent a report to five subscribers that falsely and grossly misrepresented Greenmoss Builders, Inc.'s assets and liability.[165] The report also indicated that Greenmoss voluntarily filed for bankruptcy protection.[166] Greenmoss notified Dunn & Bradstreet that its report was false.[167] After verifying the report's falsity, Dunn & Bradstreet "issued a corrective notice . . . to the five subscribers who had received the initial report.[168] However, Dunn and Bradstreet, Inc. denied Greenmoss's request for the names of those who had received the report.[169] Greenmoss brought an action for libel in Vermont state court.[170] A jury awarded Greenmoss $50,000 in compensatory or presumed damages and $300,000 in punitive damages.[171]

The *Dunn & Bradstreet* Court considered the reduced constitutional value of speech on matters of purely private concern, as opposed to speech on matters of public concern.[172] The Court affirmed the state's interest to compensate "private individuals for injury to their reputation."[173] In rejecting the application of *Gertz* to the punitive damage award, the Court held that Greenmoss's credit report did not concern any issue of public interest.[174] Instead, the information contained in the report constituted speech that was solely in the individual interest of Dunn & Bradstreet, the speaker, and its specific business audience, which included the five subscribers.[175] As such, on the issue of actual, presumed, and punitive damages Dunn & Bradstreet was not entitled to the special protection provided by the *New York Times* privilege.

Idaho Defamation and Libel Cases Against the Media After *New York Times v. Sullivan*

Weeks v. M-P Publications, Inc.[176] was the first Idaho Supreme Court decision after *New York Times v. Sullivan* that involved a defamation claim against the media. This case involved a front-page editorial published in the North Side News about S.N. Weeks, Walter C. Benzinger, and Elwin L. Tinker, who were all members of the Jerome City Council.[177]The editorial concerned the firing of Jerome's police chief and accused the men of being "teeny tyrants" and "three stooges."[178] The plaintiffs only alleged that they suffered general damages and did not make any claims for special damages.[179] The court recognized that prior to *New York Times*, Idaho allowed libel actions "without a plea of special damages" where a plaintiff could "establish that the words complained of were libelous per se."[180] However, the court acknowledged that *New York Times* created a "qualified privilege of 'fair comment' upon the conduct and qualifications of public officials."[181] Moreover, Idaho law subsumed the broad First Amendment protection for publishers "against false statements of fact, provided they were made without 'malice,' i. e., a knowledge of its falsity or a reckless disregard of its truth or falsity."[182]

Despite the new First Amendment concepts recognized by the Idaho Supreme Court, the analysis in *Weeks* mirrored the court's pre-*New York Times* previous approach. Specifically, the court in *Weeks* examined the editorial to determine whether the alleged defamation was libel per se.[183] The court held that the language used in the editorial was plain and unambiguous, and thus the question of whether it constituted libel per se was an issue of law that could be resolved by the court.[184] Reflecting its prior jurisprudence, including *Jenness*, *Gough I*, and

Gough II, the Idaho Supreme Court affirmed that neither hyperbole, ribaldry, nor caricature were sufficient to establish a public official or public figure's claim for a libel against the media.[185] The court in *Weeks* characterized the words at issue as political epithets and hyperbole within the scope of freedom of expression protected by the First Amendment.[186]

Bandelin v. Pietsch[187] was the first case to provide clarity about who was a public figure for purposes of Idaho libel claims against the media. This 1977 case involved Glenn Bandelin, who was a North Idaho attorney and former member of the state legislature.[188] A court appointed Bandelin to be the guardian of the person and estate of Muriel Talbot, who had been found incompetent.[189] For more than a year after Talbot's death, Bandelin failed to initiate a final accounting of Talbot's estate.[190] Another court had found that Bandelin's delay constituted "negligence in the extreme" and ordered the initiation of contempt proceedings.[191] The Sandpoint News-Bulletin reported 17 times on the proceedings.[192] Two of those reports contained misstatements, but otherwise the coverage was truthful and accurate.[193] The Sandpoint News-Bulletin prevailed in the trial court on a motion for summary judgment.[194] The Idaho Supreme Court upheld the trial court's dismissal even though the Sandpoint News-Bulletin's coverage was "unjustifiably sensational" and undeserving of applause.[195]

The court in *Bandelin* acknowledged that "a citizen's participation in community and professional affairs [does not] automatically render him a public figure."[196] Instead, the court looked to *Gertz*, which reduced "the public-figure question to a more meaningful context by looking to the nature and extent of an individual's participation in the particular controversy giving rise to the defamation."[197]

The *Bandelin* court ultimately found that Bandelin was a public figure for purposes of the First Amendment.[198] Bandelin "was prominent in the local politics of Bonner County, had been a representative in the state legislature, was a leading attorney, and was well-known throughout the county."[199] The court acknowledged that "a public figure can revert back to the 'lawful and unexciting life lead by the great bulk of the community'" and that "in recent years Bandelin's public role has subsided-that he has reverted to the 'simple small-town lawyer he was before he gained notoriety.'"[200] But rarely does a public figure shed the "residual elements of his former status even when he returns to private life."[201] Bandelin, as the guardian of Talbot's estate, "was the center of the controversy that gave rise to the Sandpoint News-Bulletin's publications."[202] Under such circumstances, Bandelin was not "just an attorney handling the probate affairs of a client,"[203] he was a pivotal figure in a public controversy: that of a court appointed guardian's accounting of an estate.[204]

Bandelin also recognized that a personal desire to retain the anonymity of a private citizen could not be outcome determinative because public figure status "does not hinge upon an individual's preference in the matter."[205] While most public figures "will have become such by the active pursuit of the limelight," the *New York Times* privilege does not hinge on whether an individual voluntarily pursued "public acclaim."[206] Instead, the actual malice standard "is based upon a value judgment that debate on public issues should be uninhibited."[207] That value "judgment is applicable to both the individual who becomes embroiled in a public controversy through no effort of his own and the individual who actively generates controversy-both abdicate their anonymity."[208]

Thirteen years after *Bandelin*, the Idaho Supreme Court in *Wiemer v. Rankin*[209] acknowledge another type of status that applies in libel actions against the media: that of "limited public figure." *Wiemer v. Rankin* represents the Idaho Supreme Court's resistance to the theory that private individuals "automatically become public figures by becoming involved in or associated with a matter that attracts public attention."[210] Instead, individuals could become "public figure for the limited purpose of comment on his connection with or involvement in, the particular controversy."[211] *Wiemer v. Rankin* involved the publication of an article written by Ronald Rankin that he distributed in a free Kootenai County tabloid.[212] The article ridiculed the prosecution's failure to conduct an inquest in to the death of Irving Weimer's wife.[213] In the article, Rankin intimated that detectives investigating the case provided him with private facts that proved that Weimer murdered his wife and that the prosecutor botched the case.[214]

Wiemer explored the content of publications much deeper than prior Idaho cases, including those before and after the application of First Amendment principles to state law claims for defamation. The court distinguished between publications of fact and publications of opinion.[215] The court reasoned that no constitutional value was assigned to false statements of fact because neither "the intentional lie nor the careless error materially advances society's interest in "'uninhibited, robust, and wide-open' debate on public issues."[216] Because there was "no such thing as a false idea,"[217] full constitutional protection applied to publications of opinion.[218] An exception to this rule exists where the author implies first-hand knowledge or possession of facts that are unknown to the public.[219] Because Ronald Rankin's publication implied reliance on statements from law enforcement that went beyond the public record, Rankin could not claim that his statements were part of an official public record or proceedings.[220] The court held that Irving Wiemer was a private figure, thus proof of actual malice was not required to recover actual damages.[221] However because the publication involved an issue of public concern, under *Gertz v. Robert Welch, Inc.*, Irving Wiemer did have to prove actual malice to recover presumed and punitive damages.[222]

One other post-*New York Times* Idaho libel case against the media, *Steele v. Spokesman-Review*,[223] discusses the sufficiency of evidence to meet the First Amendment's heightened standard. This case involved a publication in The Spokesman-Review about Edgar Steele, who filed a notice of substitution of counsel to represent several members of the Aryan Nation in a civil cause of action for assault.[224] The Spokesman-Review reported that Steele was previously acquainted with two founders of a white supremacist group and that he moved from California to Idaho around the same time as several other members of that group.[225] After The Spokesman-Review rebuffed his request to retract the article, Steele brought a lawsuit for defamation, invasion of privacy, and intentional infliction of emotional distress.[226] The lawsuit alleged that The Spokesman-Review article contained statements that were untrue or statements that falsely depicted Steele as a white supremacist by insinuation and innuendo.[227] The lawsuit was ultimately unsuccessful, in part, because the facts disclosed in the article were not private facts, but readily available from public sources.[228] Additionally, Steele failed to present sufficient evidence to support a claim for defamation against the media.[229]

Steele establishes that media defendants in a defamation case are not required to show the "literal truth of the precise statement" that was made.[230] As long as "the defamatory charge is true in substance," the court will view "[s]light inaccuracies of expression" as immaterial.[231] In Idaho, minor inaccuracies do not amount to falsity as "long as the substance, the gist, the sting of the allegedly libelous charge be justified."[232] Steele was unable to show the contested statements were untrue because much of the evidence was contradicted.[233] Steele did take over the representation of the Aryan Nations.[234] Steele also participated in the public debate over the case.[235] Finally, Steele was unable to show that any errors contained in the publication were more than "slight inaccuracies."[236]

Clark v. Spokesman-Review[237] represents one of the final Idaho cases of libel against the media that was decided after *New York Times*. This case also provides the most modern recitation of Idaho's elements for a cause of action libel and the standard of proof on such claims against the media. *Clark* involves an article that discussed Bob Nonini's drug arrest and his "involvement as a government informant for narcotics officers."[238] The State Chairman of Idaho's Republican Party, Trent Clark, "issued a press release criticizing the article and supporting Nonini, who was also a potential Republican senatorial candidate.[239] Clark and the article's author eventually discussed Nonini's case over the telephone.[240] The Spokesman Review reported several rather disparaging remarks that Clark made about African-American males during that conversation.[241] Clark ultimately brought a lawsuit for defamation and invasion of privacy.[242]

Clark looked to both pre- and post-*New York Times* jurisprudence in its analysis of the requirements of a defamation case against the media in Idaho. In this case, the Idaho Supreme Court recited the requirements of defamation as:

> "(1) communicated information concerning the plaintiff to others; (2) that the information was defamatory; and (3) that the plaintiff was damaged because of the communication. . . . As a fourth element, when a publication concerns a public official, public figure, or matters of public concern and there is a media defendant, the plaintiff must also show the falsity of the statements at issue in order to prevail in a defamation suit. Finally, if the plaintiff is a public figure, the *New York Times* . . . standard applies, and the plaintiff can recover only if he can prove actual malice, knowledge of falsity or reckless disregard of truth, by clear and convincing evidence."[243]

The court found that Clark was a public figure and thus the *New York Times* privilege applied against his claim for defamation.[244] As a result, Clark was required to show actual malice in order to recover damages.[245]

The *Clark* court provided a lengthy and comprehensive interpretation of the approach to the actual malice standard:

> "Actual malice is not defined as an evil intent or a motive arising from spite. In a defamation action, actual malice is knowledge of falsity or reckless disregard of truth. Mere negligence is insufficient; the plaintiff must demonstrate that 'the author in fact entertained serious doubts as to the truth of his publication or acted with a high degree of awareness of ... probable falsity.' The standard of actual malice is a subjective one. However, although actual malice is a subjective standard, self-interested denials of actual malice from the defendant can be rebutted with other evidence. This Court focuses on whether there is sufficient evidence of purposeful avoidance of the truth."[246]

Clark designated "clear and convincing evidence" as the standard that applies to Idaho defamation cases against the media.[247] Ultimately, Clark was unable to show the exact wording of his reported statement was false.[248]

Clark testified in a deposition that he could not "remember word for word what he said," but he was certain the author took his statements out of context.[249] Clark's testimony was neither clear nor convincing on the question of whether reporter "had knowledge of the alleged falsity of the reported statement" or that the reporter "engaged in reckless falsification."[250]

Conclusion

Idaho, like most states, recognizes libel and slander as types of claims for defamation. Due to the nature of news media, most Idaho defamation cases are claims for libel, not slander. Libel is defined in Idaho Code 18-4801, which applies to both criminal and civil cases. Most of the early Idaho defamation cases against the media hinged on the whether the alleged publication libel per se, which alleviates the plaintiff of the burden special damages. However both the *Restatement (Second) of Torts* and the First Amendment privilege announced in *New York Times v. Sullivan* greatly influence libel law in Idaho. The *New York Times* privilege requires a public official or figure to prove "actual malice" to recover damages in a defamation claim against the media. Where the alleged defamation is of public concern, the privilege requires a private individual to prove actual malice to recover presumed and punitive damages. One should note that even after *New York Times*, the analysis in Idaho defamation cases against the media continu to hinge on whether an alleged publication was libelous per se. Very little suggests that trend will discontinue in the future.

Endnotes

1 Dwyer v. Libert, 30 Idaho 576 (1917).

2 *Restatement (Second) of Torts* § 568 (Am. Law Inst. 1975).

3 *Id.* at §§ 559, 564.

4 *Id.* at § 568(2); *see also id.* at § 568 cmt. d.

5 *Id.* at § 568(1); *see also id.* at § 568 cmt. d-f.

6 *Id.* at § 568A; *see also id.* at § 568 cmt. d-f.

7 Idaho Code § 18-4801.

8 Sweeney v. Capital News Pub. Co., 37 F. Supp. 355, 356 (D. Idaho 1941).

9 37 F. Supp. 355 (D. Idaho 1941)

10 *Id.*

11 60 Idaho 326 (1939).

12 *O'Malley*, 60 Idaho at 328-37.

13 *Id.* at 337.

14 *Id.* at 336.

15 *Id.* at 330.

16 *Id.*

17 *Id.* at 330-37.

18 *Restatement (Second) of Torts* § 558 (Am. Law Inst. 1975).

19 *Id.* at § 568(1) & (2).

20 *Id.* at § 568A.

21 *Id.* at § 568A cmt. a.

22 *Id.* at § 568A cmt. b.

23 *Id.* at § 560.

24 *Id.* at §§ 564A.

25 *Id.* at §§ 561 & 562.

26 *Id.* at §§ 565 & 566.

27 *Id.* at § 559.

28 *Id.* at § 565 cmt. a.

29 *Id.* at § 566.

30 *Id.* at §§ 581A & 583.

31 *See Id.* at §§ 585-612.

32 *Id.* at § 577.

33 *See generally id.* at § 652D cmt. a & *id.* at § 577.

34 *Id.* at § 652D cmt. a. *See also id.* at § 577.

35 *Id.* at § 652D cmt. a.

36 *Id.*

37 *Id.*

38 *Id.* at § 577A.

39 *Id.*

40 *Id.*

41 *Id.* at § 578.

42 *Id.* at §§ 569-76.

43 *Id.* at § 621.

44 *Id.* at § 621 cmt. a.

45 *Id.* at § 569.

46 *Id.* at § 621 cmt. a.

47 *Id.* at § 569 cmt. a-c.

48 *Id.*

49 U.S. CONST. amend. I.

50 Weeks v. M-P Publications, 95 Idaho 634, 637 (1973).

51 376 U.S. 254 (1964).

52 *New York Times*, 376 U.S. at 279-80.

53 *Id.* at 280.

54 30 Idaho 576 (1917).

55 *Dwyer*, 30 Idaho at 582.

56 *Id.*

57 *Id.*

58 *Id.*

59 36 Idaho 697 (1923).

60 *Jenness*, 36 Idaho at 701-02.

61 *Id.* at 700.

62 *Id.* at 702.

63 *Id.*

64 *Id.*

65 *Id.* at 702-03.

66 *Id.* at 703.

67 *Id.*

68 Idaho Code § 18-4801.

69 73 Idaho 173 (1952).

70 *Gough I*, 73 Idaho at 176-78.

71 *Id.*

72 *Id.* at 178.

73 *Id.*

74 *Id.* at 178.

75 *Id.* at 177.

76 *Id.* at 179.

77 *Id.*

78 75 Idaho 502 (1954).

79 *Gough II*, 75 Idaho at 507-08.

80 *Id. at* 508.

81 *Id.*

82 *Id.*

83 *Gough I*, 73 Idaho at 179.

84 *Id.* at 180.

85 *Id.*

86 *Id.* at 178.

87 *Id.* at 510 (citing *Restatement of Torts* § 607(1)).

88 *Id.* at 510.

89 376 U.S. 254 (1964).

90 *New York Times*, 376 U.S. at 256, 264-65, 267-68.

91 *Id.* at 279-82.

92 338 U.S. 130 (1967).

93 418 U.S. 323 (1974).

94 472 U.S. 749 (1985).

95 Hustler Magazine v. Falwell, 483 U.S. 46 (1988).

96 Time, Inc. v. Hill, 385 U.S. 374 (1967).

97 *New York Times*, 376 U.S. at 256.

98 *Id.*

99 *Id.* at 256-61.

100 *Id.* at 258.

101 *Id.*

102 *Id.*

103 *Id.*

104 *Id.*

105 *Id.* at 256.

106 *Id.* at 264-65.

107 *Id.* at 269.

108 *Id.*

109 *Id.*

110 *Id.*

111 *Id.* at 279.

112 *Id.* at 279-80.

113 *Id.* at 281-82.

114 *Id.* at 270.

115 *Id.* at 283.

116 *Id.* at 283-84.

117 *Id.* at 284.

118 388 U.S. 130 (1967).

119 *Curtis Publishing Co.*, 388 U.S. at 135. *See also id.* at 135-140.

120 *Id.* at 135.

121 *Id.* at 136-37.

122 *Id.* at 137.

123 *Id.* at 138.

124 *Id.*

125 *Id.* at 140. See also id. at 140-42.

126 *Id.* at 140.

127 *Id.*

128 *Id.*

129 *Id.*

130 *Id.* at 141.

131 *Id.* at 141-42.

132 *Id.* at 153-55.

133 *Id.* at 147-48.

134 *Id.* at 149-50.

135 *Id.* at 150.

136 *Id.* at 151.

137 *Id.*

138 *Id.*

139 *Id.*

140 *Id.* at 152.

141 *Id.*

142 *Id.* at 155.

143 *Id.* at 154.

144 *Id.* at 155.

145 *Id.*

146 *Id.*

147 418 U.S. 323 (1974).

148 *Gertz*, 418 U.S. at 325. *See also id.* at 325-32.

149 *Id.* at 326.

150 *Id.*

151 *Id.*

152 *Id.* at 329.

153 *Id.* at 329-30.

154 *Id.* at 330-31.

155 *Id.* at 345-46.

156 *Id.* at 344.

157 *Id.* at 344-45.

158 *Id.* at 345.

159 *Id.* at 351.

160 *Id.* at 346 (rejecting Rosenbloom v. Metromedia, Inc., 403 U.S. 29 (1971), and its "public or general interest" test for determining the applicability of the *New York Times* privilege).

161 *Id.* at 351-53.

162 *Id.* at 349.

163 *Id.* at 349-50.

164 472 U.S. 749 (1985).

165 *Dunn & Bradstreet, Inc.*, 472 U.S. at 751.

166 *Id.*

167 *Id.*

168 *Id.* at 751-72.

169 *Id.* at 752.

170 *Id.*

171 *Id.*

172 *Id.* at 759-61.

173 *Id.* at 757.

174 *Id.* at 761-62.

175 *Id.* at 762.

176 95 Idaho 634 (1973).

177 *Weeks*, 95 Idaho at 635-36.

178 *Id.*

179 *Id.* at 636.

180 *Id.*

181 *Id.* at 637.

182 *Id.*

183 *Id.* at 636.

184 *Id.*

185 *Id.* at 638.

186 *Id.* at 638-39. In a very short opinion issued one year after *Weeks v. M-P Publications, Inc.*, the Idaho Supreme Court again dismissed a public official's claim for defamation again the media as constitutionally insufficient political epithets and hyperbole. *See Hemingway v. Fritz*, 96 Idaho 364 (1974).

187 98 Idaho 337 (1977).

188 *Bandelin*, 98 Idaho at 338.

189 *Id.*

190 *Id.*

191 *Id.*

192 *Id.*

193 *Id.*

194 *Id.* at 338-39.

195 *Id.* at 341.

196 *Id.* at 340.

197 *Id.*

198 *Id.* at 339-40.

199 *Id.* at 340.

200 *Id.*

201 *Id.*

202 *Id.*

203 *Id.*

204 *Id.*

205 *Id.*

206 *Id.*

207 *Id.*

208 *Id.*

209 117 Idaho 566 (1990).

210 *Wiemer,* 117 Idaho at 570-71.

211 *Id.* at 570.

212 *Id.* at 567.

213 *Id.* at 568-69.

214 *Id.*

215 *Id.* at 571-72.

216 *Id.* at 571.

217 *Id.*

218 *Id.* at 572.

219 *Id.* at 571-72.

220 *Id.* at 571-73.

221 *Id.* at 573-74.

222 *Id.*

223 138 Idaho 249 (2002).

224 *Steele,* 138 Idaho at 250-51.

225 *Id.* at 250.

226 *Id.*

227 *Id.*

228 *Id.* at 253.

229 *Id.* at 252-53.

230 *Id.* at 253.

231 *Id.*

232 *Id.*

233 *Id.*

234 *Id.*

235 *Id.*

236 *Id.*

237 144 Idaho 427 (2007).

238 *Clark*, 144 Idaho at 429.

239 *Id.*

240 *Id.*

241 *Id.*

242 *Id.*

243 *Id.* at 430.

244 *Id.*

245 *Id.*

246 *Id.* at 431.

247 *Id.* at 430.

248 *Id.* at 431-32.

249 *Id.* at 432.

250 *Id.* For the same reasons, Clark's testimony was also insufficient on his claim for invasion of privacy by false light. *Id.* at 432-33.

Chapter 5

Obscenity and Indecency

By Shaakirrah R. Sanders
Associate Professor of Law, University of Idaho

Title 18, Chapter 41 of the Idaho Code criminalizes indecency and obscenity.[1] For the media, there may be several sections of interest. First, section 18-4103, which broadly prohibits the sale or distribution of obscene materials.[2] Second, section 18-4103A, which bans the advertisement or promotion of obscene matters.[3] Third, section 18-4104, which prohibits participation in and production or presentation of live obscene conduct in a public place.[4] Fourth, section 18-4105, which prohibits the public display of offensive sexual material.[5] Finally, section 18-4113, which preempts city and county laws regulating obscene materials.[6] There are no Idaho Supreme Court cases applying Idaho's obscenity and indecency statute against the media. *Taylor v. KTVB*[7] involved the airing of a nude Oren Taylor's arrest in 1974,[8] but that case did not involve Idaho's indecency statute. That case involved claims of invasion of privacy,[9] which is discussed in Chapter 10.

Although Chapter 41 refers to indecency and obscenity, only the latter is defined. Section 18-4101(A) defines obscene material as that:

"(1) which the average person, applying contemporary community standards, would find, when considered as a whole, appeals to the prurient interest; and
(2) which depicts or describes patently offensive representations or descriptions of:
(a) ultimate sexual acts, normal or perverted, actual or simulated; or
(b) masturbation, excretory functions, or lewd exhibition of the genitals or genital area."[10]

Section 18-4101A also excludes from the definition of obscene materials those that "when considered as a whole, and in the context in which it is used, possesses serious literary, artistic, political or scientific value."[11] In addition to exclusions for materials that are of serious literary, artistic, political or scientific value, the scope of obscenity is further limited by section 18-4101(B). This section defines "prurient interest" as:

> ...a shameful or morbid interest in nudity, sex, or excretion, which goes substantially beyond customary limits of candor in description or representation of such matters. If it appears from the character of the material or the circumstances of its dissemination that the subject matter is designed for a specially susceptible audience or clearly defined deviant sexual group, the appeal of the subject matter shall be judged with reference to such audience or group.[12]

Idaho's obscenity statute includes within its scope "any individual, partnership, firm, association, corporation, or other legal entity; or any agent or servant thereof," which includes the media.[13]

Idaho's definitions of "obscenity" and "prurient interest" are direct reflections of United States Supreme Court jurisprudence. The Court first defined obscenity in *Roth v. United States*,[14] a 1957 case that questioned the federal prohibition against mailing an "obscene, lewd, lascivious, or filthy book, pamphlet, picture, paper, letter, writing, print, or other publication of indecent character."[15] Justice Brennan wrote for the majority and reflected that obscene materials were banned in the almost all of the U.S. colonies.[16] In fact, all states made blasphemy or profanity statutory crimes.[17] Massachusetts in particular criminalized publishing filthy, obscene, and profane items.[18] This reflection upon U.S. founding history was not the only reason for the Court to conclude that obscenity was among those areas of speech that the First Amendment[19] afforded less protection. The founder's goal when conceiving of the freedoms for speech and of the press was to assure "unfettered interchange of ideas" as a way of bringing about the "political and social changes desired by the people."[20] Obscenity had no redeeming social importance for U.S. constitutional purposes, which was a view shared by 50 other nation states that restrained or banned obscene speech.[21]

Roth cautioned that obscenity was not synonymous with sex.[22] Obscene materials are those that deal with sex in a manner that appeals only to *prurient interest*. In 1973, *Paris Adult Theatre I v. Slaton*[23] further delineated the line between obscenity and sex. That case questioned whether Georgia could criminally punish several theatres and their owners for charging admission to show two adult films.[24] The entrances to the theaters were conventional, inoffensive, and without any pictures.[25] However, before entering the theaters patrons were required to show identification proving they were at least 21 years of age.[26] Both films depicted sexual conduct that could only be described as "hard core pornography" that left little to the imagination.[27] Because Georgia's law was not aimed at speech, but rather "defined sexual conduct," the Court held that Georgia's legitimate interests in protecting the health and safety of minors was sufficiently related.[28]

While *Paris Adult Theatre I* upheld *Roth*'s distinction between sex and obscenity, the Court did not actually define the distinction. This failure is the subject of two dissenting opinions in that case. Justice Brennan wrote the majority opinion in *Roth v. United States*, but now argued in *Paris Adult Theatre I* that *Roth* should be overturned due to the Court's inability to reconcile obscenity jurisprudence with First Amendment principles.[29] Justice Brennan had now come to believe that obscenity was protected expressive conduct.[30] Additionally, Justice Brennan felt that proposed definitions of obscenity would necessarily be too dependent on each individual's experience, outlook, and idiosyncrasies.[31] Thus, it would be impossible to distinguish between protected and unprotected speech.[32] Justice Douglas argued that the First Amendment should not leave obscene materials unprotected.[33] Because art and literature reflect tastes, which are not reducible to precise definitions, individuals, not governments should be the judge of what is obscene and what is not obscene.[34] Otherwise, the First Amendment allows the government to act as censor, which was against the founder's intent.[35]

Miller v. California[36] provides the framework for the distinction between sex and obscenity, perhaps in response to past failures to do so. *Miller* questioned whether California could criminally punish an individual for knowingly distributing obscene matters. [37] Miller allegedly engaged in an aggressive mass mailing campaign to advertise the sale of illustrated books featuring adult content.[38] According to Chief Justice Warren E. Burger, the act of mailing amounting to thrusting unwanted materials upon "unwilling recipients who had in no way indicated a desire to receive such materials."[39] The Court held that California had "a legitimate interest in prohibiting dissemination or exhibition of obscene materials when the mode of dissemination carried a significant danger of exposure to juveniles or of offending the sensibilities of unwilling recipients."[40]

Miller extends *Paris Adult Theatre I* and *Roth* by excluding obscenity from the category of speech protected by the First and Fourteenth Amendments.[41] Nevertheless, state obscenity bans must be carefully limited to provide basic guidelines and standards to judge obscenity.[42] *Miller* announced four factors to aid in this determination:

1. Whether the average person, applying a contemporary community standard, would find that the work, taken as a whole, appeals to prurient interests[43];
2. Whether the work depicts specifically described sexual conduct[44];
3. Whether the work is patently offensive, i.e. depicts hard core sexual conduct[45]; and
4. Whether the work, taken as a whole, has no serious literary artistic, political or scientific value.[46]

As stated, Chapter 14 of the Idaho Code only defines obscenity. The First Amendment also fills the gap left in the Idaho Code, specifically Chapter 41's failure to define indecency. *Cohen v. California*,[47] a 1971 case, involved whether the First Amendment allowed California to criminally punish an individual for wearing clothing upon which profanity was printed.[48] Cohen entered an LA county courthouse wearing a jacket that visibly bared the words the words "F--- the Draft."[49] Cohen was arrested, charged, and convicted for "maliciously and willfully disturbing the peace or quiet . . . by offensive conduct."[50] Prior to his arrest, Cohen did not engage in any threatening behavior or acts of violence.[51] Nor did Cohen make loud or unusual noises.[52] Cohen testified that he wore the jacket to communicate to the public the depth of his feelings against the Vietnam War and its associated draft.[53] Justice John Marshall Harlan II led the majority's reversal of the conviction, which rested solely on the asserted offensiveness of Cohen's speech.[54]

Cohen perhaps explains Idaho's failure to address indecency. The Court pointed out that no category of unprotected speech applied to the words printed on Cohen's jacket.[55] Cohen's speech did not constitute fighting words and was not inherently likely to provoke a violent reaction.[56] Cohen was unlikely to provoke a hostile reaction from a group of persons because Cohen's speech was not violently arousing.[57] Cohen's words were neither obscene nor erotic.[58] Cohen did not communicate that he wanted to engage in sexual congress with the draft.[59] Nor did the "crudely defaced jacket" conjure a "vulgar allusion" of "psychic stimulation."[60] While California had a legitimate interest in protecting the public from offensive or crude speech, the state could not curtail all potentially offensive or indecent speech.[61] Individuals are captives outside the privacy or sanctuary of their home and have no power to silence dissonance.[62] There was no showing that the public was unable turn away from Cohen's speech by averting their eyes.[63] The Court pointed out that the First Amendment was designed to remove government restraints from public discussion.[64] As Justice Harlan puts it "[o]ne man's vulgarity is another's lyric" and "matters of taste" should be left to individuals.[65] Because linguistic expression is capable of communicating ideas *and* emotions, governments should not forbid particular words.[66] Such bans run the risk of suppressing ideas.[67]

Cohen suggests that "[s]exual expression which is indecent but not obscene is protected by the First Amendment."[68] *Cohen* does not explain why indecent language and behavior are noticeably lacking on U.S. television and radio broadcasts. *Federal Communications Commission v. Pacifica Foundation*[69] was decided in 1978 and addressed whether the First Amendment allows the federal government to regulate indecent radio broadcasts. At 2 p.m., a New York radio station owned by Pacifica Foundation aired George Carlin's 12-minute monologue entitled "Filthy Words."[70] The monologue featured Carlin repeatedly using words which had been banned on public radio by various federal statutes.[71] A listener wrote a letter to the Federal Communications Commission (FCC) after his young son had heard the broadcast. [72] Pacifica Foundation disputed whether Carlin's language was obscene and argued that listeners were warned before the broadcast.[73] The FCC issued a declaratory order granting the complaint, but did not impose formal sanctions against Pacifica.[74]

Pacifica Foundation observed that television and radio broadcasts had a uniquely pervasive presence in American lives.[75] Such speech breached the privacy guaranteed in one's home, where the right to be left alone outweighs the First Amendment right of intruders.[76] Broadcast audiences constantly tune in and out.[77] That audience includes children who can easily access the medium.[78] Children's vocabularies are instantly susceptible to influence and in this sense, a warning at the beginning of a broadcast could be ineffective.[79] Casting Carlin's speech aside as indecent, the Court held that First Amendment protections do not extend to speech that is contrary or offensive to contemporary moral standards.[80] While the offensiveness of speech is not reason alone to regulate, such speech does have a low place in the hierarchy of First Amendment values. Carlin's speech was not essential to any exposition of ideas and was of slight social value.[81] This, and the fact that Carlin's speech presented was in the medium of a radio broadcast, meant that the FCC could place a reasonable time, place, and manner restriction on that speech.[82]

The continued application of *Pacifica Foundation* against the media should be in doubt. Many local, regional, and national broadcast media outlets also post identical content on the internet. *Reno v. American Civil Liberties Union*[83] held that the First Amendment did not allow the federal government to regulate indecent speech over the internet.[84] *Reno* concerned the two federal laws that prohibited the knowing transmission of obscene or indecent material over the internet to any recipient under the age of 18 years of age.[85] The statutes also prohibited the knowing, sending, or displaying of patently offensive messages in a manner that makes such message available to a person under 18 years of age.[86] Justice John Paul Stevens distinguished the federal statutes at issue, which represented total bans on speech. Justice Stevens also wrote the majority opinion in *Pacifica Foundation* and distinguished that case as one where the regulations were limited to time.[87] Justice Stevens recognized the internet as a new medium that was not as invasive as broadcast media.[88] Justice Stevens reasoned that the risk that minors would accidentally access indecent material was too remote,[89] a suggestion that seemed plausible in 1997.

Reno v. American Civil Liberties Union posits regulation of the internet cannot suppress too large an amount of speech such that it prohibits protected speech.[90] Such a chilling effect would cause self-censorship, which is untenable under the First Amendment.[91] Justice Stevens also pointed to Congress's failure to define the terms "indecent" or "patently offensive," further exacerbating the possible censorship of internet speech.[92] This lack of precision proved fatal to both of the federal statutes at issue in *Reno*.[93] Finally, Justice Stevens noted the unprecedented scope of both statutes, which were not limited to commercial speech or commercial entities and applied to all nonprofit entitles and individuals who posted or displayed indecent messages on the internet.[94] The Court's reference to commercial speech is notable and is a topic covered in Chapter 9.

Endnotes

1 Idaho Code 18-4101 *et seq*.

2 Idaho Code 18-4103.

3 Idaho Code 18-4103A.

4 Idaho Code 18-4104.

5 Idaho Code 18-4105.

6 Idaho Code 18-4113.

7 96 Idaho 202 (1974).

8 *Taylor*, 96 Idaho at 202-03.

9 *Id.*

10 Idaho Code 18-4101(A).

11 *Id.*

12 Idaho Code 18-4101(B).

13 Idaho Code 18-4101(D).

14 354 U.S. 476 (1957).

15 *Roth*, 354 U.S. at 479 (citing 18 U.S.C. 1461).

16 *Id.* at 482-83.

17 *Id.*

18 *Id.*

19 U.S. Const. amend. I.

20 *Id.* at 484.

21 *Id.* at 484-85.

22 *Id.* at 487.

23 413 U.S. 49 (1973).

24 *Paris Adult Theatre I*, 413 U.S. at 50-53.

25 *Id.* at 52.

26 *Id.*

27 *Id.*

28 *Id.* at 69-70.

29 *Id.* at 73, 83 (Brennan, J. dissenting).

30 *Id.* at 73-114 (Brennan, J. dissenting).

31 *Id.* at 84-85 (Brennan, J. dissenting).

32 *Id.*

33 *Id.* at 70-73 (Douglas, J. dissenting).

34 *Id.* at 70. (Douglas, J. dissenting).

35 *Id.*

36 413 U.S. 15(1973).

37 *Miller*, 413 U.S. at 16-20.

38 *Id.* at 16-18.

39 *Id.* at 18.

40 *Id.* at 18-19.

41 *Id.* at 24.

42 *Id.*

43 *Id.*

44 *Id.*

45 *Id.*

46 *Id.*

47 403 U.S. 15 (1971).

48 *Cohen*, 403 U.S. at 16-18.

49 *Id.* at 16.

50 *Id.*

51 *Id.* at 16-17.

52 *Id.* at 16.

53 *Id.*

54 *Id.* at 18.

55 *Id.* 19-20.

56 *Id.* at 20.

57 *Id.*

58 *Id.*

59 *Id.*

60 *Id.*

61 *Id.*

62 *Id.* at 21.

63 *Id.*

64 *Id.* at 24.

65 *Id.* at 25.

66 *Id.* at 25-26.

67 *Id.* at 26.

68 Carey v. Population Services Int'l, 431 U.S. 678, 701 (1977).

69 438 U.S. 726 (1978).

70 *Pacifica Foundation*, 438 U.S. at 729.

71 *Id.* at 730-32.

72 *Id.* at 730.

73 *Id.* at 732-33.

74 *Id.* at 730.

75 *Id.* at 748.

76 *Id.*

77 *Id.* at 755-60 and n.2 (Powell, J. dissenting).

78 *Id.* at 734.

79 *Id.* at 748-50.

80 *Id.* at 745.

81 *Id.* at 746-47.

82 *Kovacs v. Cooper*, 336 U.S. 77 (1949).

83 521 U.S. 844 (1997).

84 *Reno*, 521 U.S. at 849.

85 *Id.*

86 *Id.* at 857-61.

87 *Id.* at 864-68.

88 *Id.* at 849-59.

89 *Id.* at 867.

90 *Id.* at 870-75.

91 *Id.* at 874, 879-80, and 885.

92 *Id.* at 845, 877.

93 *Id.*

94 *Id.* at 877.

Chapter 6

Idaho's Print Advertising Laws

By Justin Barnes, Ph.D.
Assistant Professor of Advertising

Managing freedom of speech can be a slippery slope when it comes to advertising. Nonetheless, restriction of freedom of speech is necessary when dealing with deception and false advertising. Advertising is a multi-billion dollar industry with the sole focus of informing and persuading consumers to make informed purchases of products and services. The industry involves creative genius that can benefit the consumers; however, advertising may not always have the best intention for the consumers' wellbeing.

When thinking of advertising and marketing law, it could be referred to as a process that manages the proper conduct of communication information toward potential consumers for a product or service. There have been multiple instances where the process goes awry, and outside parties challenge the current status of that process. Every business has the right to market and advertise its product and service, but when that activity becomes untruthful or deceptive, consumers need to be protected.

There are several areas which are protected by Idaho state law. With help from the Federal Trade Commission and Bureau of Alcohol, Tobacco, Firearms and Explosives, the laws attempt to halt false claims, fraudulent, misleading or deceptive claims, promoting illegal actions, promoting activities harmful to public health or safety, and attempting to injure the competition unfairly. The Federal Trade Commission also assists in the effort to manage advertising and marketing content in Idaho through the oversight of interstate trade practices that may have direct effect on the state. Such regulation from the Federal Trade Commission may include how a business labels its products, conducts email and telemarketing campaigns, and claims related to results the products might have on one's health or the environment.

The foundation of advertising and marketing law enforcement must focus on truth in trade practices. These are the laws regulating how businesses relate the benefits of their products to the general public ("Advertising Law," 2013). Examples of these laws include prohibitions against unreasonable health claims (e.g., that a pill will make one fit and beautiful), violations of others trademarks, or representations about the environmental impact of a product (e.g., claiming that a product is made of recycled materials when it is not) ("Advertising Law," 2013).

Of course there are federal laws which supersede state statutes. Linder (2016) states that federal preemption stems from the Supremacy Clause of the Constitution, which states the "Constitution and the laws of the United States ... shall be the supreme law of the land ... anything in the constitutions or laws of any State to the contrary notwithstanding."

Basically, it means that federal law or even a federal regulation reigns supreme over any conflicting state law.

According to Linder (2016), preemption can be either expressed or implied. To delve deeper, if Congress decides to expressly preempt state law, courts need to determine if federal law can preempt the challenged state law. Nonetheless, implied preemption is often more challenging to determine, especially when the state law does not directly clash with federal law. According to Linder, the court has to examine beyond the expressed language of federal statutes to establish whether Congress has "occupied the field" in which the state is attempting to regulate, or whether a state law directly conflicts with federal law, or whether enforcement of the state law might frustrate federal purposes.

Linder (2016) states that federal "occupation of the field" occurs, according to the Court in *Pennsylvania v Nelson* (1956), when there is "no room" left for state regulation. Courts are to look to the pervasiveness of the federal scheme of regulation, the federal interest at stake, and the danger of frustration of federal goals in making the determination as to whether a challenged state law can stand.

There are advertising laws specific to the state of Idaho.

Advertising and marketing law is a constantly evolving platform, with new challenges regularly occurring. It is an unspoken rule that media are not responsible for the content of advertising or policing the industry. The theory is that it is impossible to conduct extensive background checks to challenge the legitimacy of advertising content and the information to which it pertains. Nonetheless, the media needs to be vigilant and willing to correct and challenge false or misleading advertising to protect itself against any liability. The question remains, how much free speech is protected by the First Amendment for advertising?

In 1980, Idaho tested the federal foundation in *State of Idaho ex rel. Wayne Kidwell, Attorney General v. Master Distributors,* 101 Idaho 447. In short, the court upheld the Idaho Consumer Protection Act, and clarified its interplay with FTC standards. The case involved a scheme by a company that heavily marketed overpriced water softeners to consumers around the state. The Idaho Supreme Court decision also held that restitution could be ordered to all 300 to 400 consumers affected by the scheme, not just the 15 who testified at trial. The court noted that the purpose of the Consumer Protection Act was to protect the consumer and business against unfair advertising which may lead to unfair competition. The act also provided that one cannot advertise a service being sold at an inflated price with a false reduction as a special offer.

Idaho Consumer Protection Act—Unfair Methods and Practices, Idaho Code, Section 48-603, identifies and explains the protocol for identifying deceptive claims as follows:

> (1) Passing off goods or services as those of another;
> (2) Causing likelihood of confusion or of misunderstanding as to the source, sponsorship, approval, or certification of goods or services;
> (3) Causing likelihood of confusion or of misunderstanding as to affiliation, connection, or association with, or certification by, another;
> (4) Using deceptive representations or designations of geographic origin in connection with goods or services;
> (5) Representing that goods or services have sponsorship, approval, characteristics, ingredients, uses, benefits, or quantities that they do not have or that a person has a sponsorship, approval, status, affiliation, connection, qualifications or license that he does not have;
> (6) Representing that goods are original or new if they

are deteriorated, altered, reconditioned, reclaimed, used, or secondhand;

(7) Representing that goods or services are of a particular standard, quality, or grade, or that goods are of a particular style or model, if they are of another;

(8) Disparaging the goods, services, or business of another by false or misleading representation of fact;

(9) Advertising goods or services with intent not to sell them as advertised;

(10) Advertising goods or services with intent not to supply reasonably expectable public demand, unless the advertisement discloses a limitation of quantity;

(11) Making false or misleading statements of fact concerning the reasons for, existence of, or amounts of price reductions;

(12) Obtaining the signature of the buyer to a contract when it contains blank spaces to be filled in after it has been signed;

(13) Failing to deliver to the consumer at the time of the consumer's signature a legible copy of the contract or of any other document which the seller or lender has required or requested the buyer to sign, and which he has signed, during or after the contract negotiation;

(14) Making false or misleading statements of fact concerning the age, extent of use, or mileage of any goods;

(15) Promising or offering to pay, credit or allow to any buyer or lessee, any compensation or reward in consideration of his giving to the seller or lessor the names of prospective purchasers or lessees, or otherwise aiding the seller or lessor in making a sale or lease to another person, if the earning of the rebate, discount or other value is contingent upon the occurrence of an event subsequent to the time the buyer or lessee agrees to buy or lease;

(16) Representing that services, replacements or repairs are needed if they are not needed, or providing services, replacements or repairs that are not needed;

(17) Engaging in any act or practice which is otherwise misleading, false, or deceptive to the consumer;

(18) Engaging in any unconscionable method, act or practice in the conduct of trade or commerce, as provided in

section 48-603C, Idaho Code, provided, however, that the provisions of this subsection shall not apply to a regulated lender as that term is defined in section 28-41-301, Idaho Code;

(19) Taking advantage of a disaster or emergency declared by the governor under chapter 10, title 46, Idaho Code, or the president of the United States under the provisions of the disaster relief act of 1974, 42 U.S.C. section 5121 et seq., by selling or offering to sell to the ultimate consumer fuel or food, pharmaceuticals, or water for human consumption at an exorbitant or excessive price; provided however, this subsection shall apply only to the location and for the duration of the declaration of emergency. In determining whether a price is exorbitant or excessive, the court shall take into consideration the facts and circumstances including, but not limited to:

(a) A comparison between the price paid by the alleged violator for the fuel, food, pharmaceuticals, or water and the price for which the alleged violator sold those same items to the ultimate consumer immediately before and after the period specified by the disaster or emergency declaration;

(b) Additional costs of doing business incurred by the alleged violator because of the disaster or emergency;

(c) The duration of the disaster or emergency declaration.

Notwithstanding anything to the contrary contained elsewhere in the act, no private cause of action exists under this subsection.

In addition, the Consumer Protection Act regulates telephone solicitations and forbids deceptive practices by solicitors, in Idaho Code 48-603A. The act also discusses unconscionable methods, acts or practices in trade or commerce (Idaho Code 48-603C):

8-603C. UNCONSCIONABLE METHODS, ACTS OR PRACTICES. (1) Any unconscionable method, act or practice in the conduct of any trade or commerce violates the

provisions of this chapter whether it occurs before, during, or after the conduct of the trade or commerce.
(2) In determining whether a method, act or practice is unconscionable, the following circumstances shall be taken into consideration by the court:
(a) Whether the alleged violator knowingly or with reason to know, took advantage of a consumer reasonably unable to protect his interest because of physical infirmity, ignorance, illiteracy, inability to understand the language of the agreement or similar factor;
(b) Whether, at the time the consumer transaction was entered into, the alleged violator knew or had reason to know that the price grossly exceeded the price at which similar goods or services were readily available in similar transactions by similar persons, although price alone is insufficient to prove an unconscionable method, act or practice;
(c) Whether the alleged violator knowingly or with reason to know, induced the consumer to enter into a transaction that was excessively one-sided in favor of the alleged violator;
(d) Whether the sales conduct or pattern of sales conduct would outrage or offend the public conscience, as determined by the court.

As mentioned in the *Kidwell Court*, Idaho's Unfair Sales Act, Idaho Code 48-401 to 48-413, protects consumers against goods being sold at unfair prices. Basically, the act prohibits items being sold at low cost to attract support. The idea behind the act is to protect businesses, including farmers, who are selling goods at the fair market value. In addition, the act protects employees from working in less than desirable working conditions and for lower wages that may lead to economic depression. The act also protects against monopolization of markets. Idaho also has a Universal Commercial Code (Idaho Code Title 28), which requires buyers and sellers to be honest with language while engaging in bargaining and transaction.

Rebates Unlawful

In Idaho Code 48-413, the Unfair Sales Act, protects businesses and consumers from special rebates. The Act specifically states:

> … selling merchandise at less than cost and unfair competition contrary to public policy shall embrace any scheme of special rebates, collateral contracts or any device of any nature by and among wholesalers, retailers and direct sellers whereby such rebates or agreements are, in substance or fact, effected in violation of the spirit and intent of this chapter. It is hereby declared to be unlawful, unfair competition … for any wholesaler, retailer or direct seller to give or receive special rebates or be a party to any such agreements or devices.

Advertising and Public Health

Most commonly this affects alcohol sales within the state. Although the state liquor dispensary does not have to abide by the parameters of the law, Idaho Code 23-607 states that there shall be no form of public advertising of liquor within the state. With that noted, businesses can advertise "Happy Hour" or "2 for 1 Specials," just as long as there is no mention of alcohol sales with the advertisement.

In addition, drink types, prices and discounts are permissible to advertise inside an establishment, as long as this cannot be viewed from the outside. However, all external promotion of specific drink types, brands, prices and discounts is restricted. For example, restaurants may not post on Facebook that they are offering $4 margaritas or run a radio commercial stating that they give a $2 discount on highball drinks from 4 to 6 p.m.

Billboards and Highway Advertising

Interestingly, the state of Idaho granted cities the right to regulate the number of billboards that could be erected. In *Lamar Corporation v. City of Twin Falls*, the court ruled in favor of Twin Falls, stating that its aesthetic appearance is of substantial governmental interest. Thus, how many, and where billboards are located falls under the city's jurisdiction. Under the ordinance the city of Twin Falls created a zoning plan for other cities to possibly follow, which determines:

> (1) That the location and placement of the sign will not endanger motorists.
> (2) That the sign will not cover or blanket any prominent view of a structure or facade of historical or architectural significance.
> (3) That the sign will not obstruct views of users of adjacent buildings to side yards, front yards or to open space.
> (4) That the sign will not negatively impact the visual quality of a public open space as a public recreation facility, square, plaza, courtyard and the like.
> (5) That the sign is compatible with building heights of the existing neighborhood and does not impose a foreign or inharmonious element to an existing skyline.
> (6) That the sign's lighting will not cause hazardous or unsafe driving conditions for motorists.

Highways and Bridges Advertising

The state of Idaho has gone to lengthy effort to protect the beauty of its roads, scenic byways, and bridges from over saturations of outdoor advertising. The state legislature clearly states that advertising is for commercial purposes and that Idaho's highways and bridges need to be regulated. Idaho Code 40-1901, Beautification of Highways, states that "advertising devices" must be regulated to preserve interests ranging from safety to scenic beauty."

For businesses that are granted permission for outdoor advertising, Idaho Code 40-1909(c) states that each advertiser must display a name and an identification plate. The code also states that placing an advertising display without having a plate is in violation I.C. 40-1909, and will be subject to fine and advertisement removal.

Though there are some areas in which outdoor advertising is allowed, there are definite locations where they are not permitted. Idaho Code 40-1910(c) specifically states they are not allowed in the following:

> (1) Within the right-of-way of any highway;
> (2) Visible from any interstate or primary highway and simulating or imitating any directional, warning, danger or information sign permitted under the provisions of this chapter, or if intended or likely to be construed as giving warnings of traffic;
> (3) Within any stream or drainage canal or below the flood water level of any stream or drainage canal where the advertising display might be deluged by flood waters and swept under any highway structure crossing the stream or drainage canal or against the supports of the highway structure;
> (4) Not maintained in a safe condition;
> (5) Visible from any interstate or primary highway and displaying any red, blue or blinking intermittent light likely to be mistaken for a warning or danger signal;
> (6) Illuminated with such brilliance and so positioned as to blind or dazzle the vision of travelers on adjacent interstate or primary highways;
> (7) Purported to direct the movement of traffic;
> (8) Painted, affixed or attached to any natural feature as more particularly prohibited by section 18-7017, Idaho Code;

(9) Hinder the clear, unobstructed view of approaching or merging traffic, nor obscure from view any traffic sign or other official sign;
(10) Located as to obscure the view of any connecting highway or intersection; and
(11) Not clear or in good repair.

With Idaho Code 40-1910 in place, Idaho Code 40-1910A states the removal of legal off-premises outdoor advertising is prohibited without compensation:

> No governmental entity, including the state, or any municipality, county or other political subdivision shall remove or cause to be removed any legally placed off-premises outdoor advertising without paying compensation in cash or other method of payment mutually agreed upon, to the owner of the off-premises outdoor advertising based upon the fair market value of the off-premises outdoor advertising removed or proposed to be removed.

Product Protection Advertising Laws

Idaho has also addressed the right to protect the promotion of quality goods and services within the state, mainly agriculture products. For instance, the Idaho Potato Commission has issued strict guidelines for the promotion of potatoes within the state. In addition, there are several other commissions that oversee the protection of promotion for goods such as lentils, beans, peas, wheat, apples, cherries, honey, hops, garbanzos, alfalfa, beef, rapeseed, dairy, etc.

As an example of these commission jurisdictions, the Idaho Potato Commission is authorized and directed, in Idaho Code 22-1208, to disseminate information in these areas:

> (a) Relating to potatoes and the importance thereof in

preserving the public health, the economy thereof in the diet of the people and the importance thereof in the nutrition of children;

(b) Relating to the manner, method and means used and employed in the production, transportation, promotion and grading of potatoes and to laws of the state regulating and safeguarding such production, transportation, promotion and grading;

I Relating to the added cost to the producer and dealer in producing and handling potatoes to meet the high standards imposed by the state that insure a pure and wholesome product;

(d) Relating to the effect upon the public health which would result from a breakdown of the Idaho potato industry;

(e) Relating to the reasons why producers and dealers should receive a reasonable return on their labor and investment;

(f) Relating to the problem of furnishing the consumer at all times with an abundant supply of fine quality potatoes at reasonable prices;

(g) Relating to factors of instability peculiar to the vegetable industry in general, and the potato industry in particular, such as unbalanced production, effect of the weather, influence of consumer purchasing power and price relative to the cost of other items of food in the normal diet of people, all to the end that an intelligent and increasing consumer demand may be created;

(h) Relating to the possibilities of increased consumption of Idaho potatoes;

(i) Relating to such other, further and additional information as shall tend to promote increased consumption of Idaho potatoes, as may foster a better understanding and more efficient cooperation between producers, dealers and the consuming public;

(j) Relating to branding, labeling, stenciling, sealing or packaging to promote and use Idaho potatoes and to protect their identity as far as possible to the final consumer.

Dairy is the most heavily protected when firms choose promotional activities that use words such as cream, butter, cheese, dairy, cow, milk, butter, etc. In addition, Idaho Code 37-1003B was initiated to oversee the unfair selling of dairy products, stating:

> (a) The payment, allowance, or acceptance of secret rebates, secret refunds, or unearned discounts, whether in the form of money or otherwise, except as provided in paragraph (i) of this section.
> (b) The giving of any milk, cream, dairy products, services, money, or articles of any kind except to bona fide charities for the purpose of securing or retaining the milk, cream, or dairy products business of any wholesale customer; provided, however, that nothing herein shall be construed to prohibit a distributor of frozen dairy products, frozen dessert and frozen novelties, for reasonable compensation as provided in section 37-1003c, from furnishing a wholesale customer with, and maintaining such refrigeration facilities as shall be reasonably necessary for the storage and preservation of the frozen products distributed by such distributor to such wholesale customer; provided further, that the use of said refrigeration facilities by any person for the storage or preservation of any product other than the frozen products distributed to said wholesale customer by the distributor furnishing such facilities shall be an unfair and unlawful business practice.
> (c) The extension to any wholesale customer or consumer of special prices or services not made available to all wholesale customers or consumers who purchase milk, cream, or dairy products of like quantity under like terms and conditions.
>
> 1. No payment, credit, or compensation may lawfully be allowed by a distributor to a wholesale customer for advertising or display in connection with the sale of a distributor's milk, cream, or dairy product.
> 2. No payment of money, or payment, or gift, or loan of anything of value may lawfully be given to a wholesale customer for the privilege of painting or placing a sign, advertisement, or other advertising material, or otherwise advertising a distributor's products in, on, or adjoining any premises selling milk, cream or dairy products.

3. No outside advertising material permissible under this section may lawfully advertise items other than the distributor's milk, cream, and dairy products, and items made from the same, except not more than one-third (1/3) of the space on such advertising material may be allocated to the wholesale customer's name and products served in conjunction with milk, cream, and dairy products.

4. Inside advertising material furnished by a distributor of frozen dairy products shall be confined and limited to the advertising of the frozen dairy products manufactured by and/or distributed by the manufacturer or distributor of said frozen dairy products and/or their agents and may include the name, brands and description of the frozen dairy products of said manufacturer or distributor. Provided, further, that not more than one-third (1/3) of the space on such advertising material may be allocated to the wholesale customer's name and products served in conjunction with milk, cream, and dairy products.

(d) Any false or misleading advertising of milk, cream or dairy products.

(e) Discriminations in price between wholesale customers, or between consumers, who purchase milk, cream, or dairy products of like grade and quality under like conditions of service where the effect of such discrimination may be substantially to lessen competition or to injure or destroy or prevent competition with the person who either grants or knowingly receives the benefit of such discrimination; provided, that nothing herein shall prevent differentials which make only due allowance for differences in the cost of the raw product used in such milk, cream, or dairy products, or the cost of manufacture, processing, sale or delivery resulting from the different methods or quantities in which said commodities are manufactured, processed, sold or delivered.

(f) The sale of milk, cream, and dairy products at less than cost which, as used herein, shall mean the cost of raw product, plus all costs of manufacturing, processing, handling, sale and delivery, including overhead costs. Evidence of

cost, based on impartial audits or surveys, made within a reasonable time prior to an alleged violation of this subparagraph shall constitute prima facie proof of such cost at the time of the commission of such violation.
(g) False statements or representations, knowingly made, by any wholesale customer or consumer, or anyone acting on the behalf of either, to any distributor or manufacturer, or any representative thereof, that a competitor or such distributor or manufacturer has offered or is offering to sell, or is selling milk, cream, or dairy products to said wholesale customer or consumer at a lower price or prices than said manufacturer or distributor has offered or is offering to sell, or is selling the same, or that said competitor has offered or is offering to do, or is doing any of the business practices heretofore declared to be unfair and unlawful.
(h) The making or renewal of any money loans to any wholesale customer.
(i) The provisions of this chapter shall not prohibit the use of a discount coupon or the giving of an article in connection with the sale of dairy products to consumers, provided in doing so, the price of the dairy product is not lowered below its cost.

Medical Advertising

Under Idaho Code 18-603 it is unlawful for anyone other than a physician or medical entity to advertise services for abortion or contraception. The law states:

> Every person, except licensed physicians of this state and those licensed or registered health care providers hereinafter referred to acting under their direct supervision or medical order, who willfully publishes any notice or advertisement of any medicine or means for producing or facilitating a miscarriage or abortion, or for the prevention of conception, or who offers his services by any notice, advertisement, or otherwise to assist in the accomplishment of any such purpose, is guilty of a felony. A licensed physician or licensed or registered health care provider acting at his direction or medical order may lawfully provide examina-

tions, prescriptions, devices and informational materials regarding prevention of conception to any person requesting the same who, in the good faith judgment of the physician or such provider, is sufficiently intelligent and mature to understand the nature and significance thereof.

Professional Trade Name Advertising

As mentioned previously in the chapter, the Uniform Commercial Code requires that sellers be honest with language while engaging in bargaining and transaction. Naturally, this becomes an issues with auto sales in the state. Idaho Code 49-1613 states that dealers cannot intentionally publish or circulate misleading advertisements for the products being sold by the licensed dealer.

In addition to the Uniform Commercial Code, the Lanham Act, a federal statute, is designed to protect consumers against misleading advertisements as well. The Lanham Act also addresses the issues of trademarks, and is considered the cousin to Idaho's Registration and Protection of Trademarks Act (Idaho Code 48-5), which permits a lawsuit against another party diluting the value of a trademark. Under Idaho Code 48-513, there are criteria the court needs to consider to determine if there was in fact dilution and harm to another business's trademark:

(1) The degree of inherent or acquired distinctiveness of the mark in this state;
(2) The duration and extent of use of the mark in connection with the goods and services;
(3) The duration and extent of advertising and publicity of the mark in this state;
(4) The geographical extent of the trading area in which the mark is used;
(5) The channels of trade for the goods or services with which the owner's mark is used;

(6) The degree of recognition of the owner's mark in its and in the other's trading areas and channels of trade in this state; and

(7) The nature and extent of use of the same or similar mark by third parties.

Qualification of Newspapers for Notice Publications

In Idaho, a carrier needs to be legally approved to carry legal notices by state law. As the statute states, newspapers need to claim geographic location. This has actually been challenged in Ketchum, Idaho, where the Wood River Journal and the Idaho Mountain Express contested each other as the newspaper for the geographic region. In this specific case, the judge ruled in favor of the Idaho Mountain Express, since its only office was located in Ketchum. The Wood River Journal also had a presence in Ketchum, but only as a satellite office. The following statute lays out the qualifications of newspaper printing within the state (Idaho Code 60-106, Qualifications of Newspapers Printing Legal Notices):

> No legal notice, advertisement or publication of any kind required or provided by the laws of the state of Idaho, to be published in a newspaper, shall be published or have any force or effect, as such, unless the same be published in a newspaper of general interest published in the state of Idaho, and which newspaper if published weekly, has been continuously and uninterruptedly published in the county during a period of seventy-eight (78) consecutive weeks prior to the first publication of the notice, or advertisement, and, if published daily, has been so published as a daily newspaper in the county during a period of twelve (12) consecutive months prior to the first publication of the notice or advertisement; provided that, notwithstanding any other provision of Idaho laws, the term "newspaper of (or having) general circulation," wherever used in Idaho

Code as a qualification of newspapers required to be used for the publication of notice, shall mean a "newspaper," as defined in this section, that is published within the boundaries of the governmental entity wherein the notice is required to be published and which newspaper has the largest paid circulation among all newspapers published in that governmental entity as verified by the sworn statement of average total paid or requested circulation for the preceding twelve (12) months that was filed on the annual statement of ownership, management and circulation with the U.S. postal service on the date immediately preceding the date of the required publication of notice; excepting that, where no newspaper is published within the governmental entity required to publish a notice, the term "newspaper of (or having) general circulation" shall mean the newspaper with the largest paid circulation published within any county in which the governmental entity is located, or the newspaper published nearest to the boundaries of the governmental entity; provided, that nothing in this chapter shall invalidate the publication of such notice or advertisement in any newspaper which has simply changed its name, frequency of publication, suspended publication because of an act of God, or public enemy, fire, strike, or other labor dispute, explosion, flood, government prohibition, government requisition of essential property, preferential government orders, breakdown, legal acts of public authorities or other acts beyond the control of the publisher for a period of not to exceed six (6) months, or changed the place of publication from one part of the county to another part thereof, without breaking the continuity of its regular issues for the required length of time: and, provided further, that this chapter shall not apply to counties in which no newspaper has been published for the required length of time: provided the term "Newspaper" as used in this section shall apply only to such newspapers of general interest made up of at least four (4) pages of at least five (5) columns each, printed from type matter or from "slugs" cast upon the linotype or intertype or similar "slug-casting" machine, or by the process known as "offset," or stereotyped forms of at least seventeen and three-fourths (17 3/4) inches depth; or, if

> smaller pages, then comprising an equivalent amount of type matter, and which shall have at least two hundred (200) bona fide subscribers living within the county in which the newspaper is published at regular intervals and, in no case, less frequently than once a week; provided that a newspaper produced by the process known as mimeographing or similar methods shall not be deemed a legal newspaper for publications of any kind. And provided further, that any duly qualified newspaper, as hereinbefore defined, shall not forfeit its standing as such by reason of the fact that it has suspended publication for all or any part of the period during which the United States has been or shall be engaged in the prosecution of any war, or for one (1) year following the date of the proclamation of the President of the United States declaring that this nation is no longer at war, or the termination of a state of war shall be otherwise established. And if any such newspaper shall resume regular publication within one (1) year from the date when the termination of the state of war shall be so established, it shall then be as fully qualified to publish any legal notice, advertisement, or publication required to be published by the laws of the state of Idaho, as if such newspaper had not suspended regular publication during the above mentioned period of time.
> No newspaper shall qualify under this section unless the same shall hold a valid second class mailing permit from the United States Post Office. Any violations of the previous requirements of this section concerning printing of newspapers other than in the governmental entity in which a notice or advertisement is required to be printed are hereby excused and any advertisement published in any such newspapers is hereby validated.

Newspapers can charge separate rates for advertising. Idaho's rates for official notices states (Idaho Code 60-105 (2)):

> On and after October 1, 2008, the rate to be charged for all official notices required by law to be published in any newspaper in this state, by any state, county, municipal official or other person, shall be as follows: eight cents (8¢)

for each pica in a column line for the first insertion and seven cents (7¢) for each pica in a column line for each subsequent insertion. For table and figure matter, the rate shall be nine cents (9¢) for each pica in a column line for the first insertion, and seven cents (7¢) for each pica in a column line for each subsequent insertion. In the event that a column line ends in a one-half (1/2) pica measurement, the rate for such one-half (1/2) pica shall be one-half (1/2) the rate established for a full pica for the type of matter set forth herein. For purposes of this section, the type used shall not be smaller than seven (7) point nor greater than eight (8) point. (Idaho Code 60-105(2)).

Promoting Confidence in Politics

Similarly, Idaho requires that all contributions to political advertising must be made available to the public for transparency. Providing public access to this kind of information about the flow of money in politics empowers oversight and accountability in the government decision-making process. While many municipalities release some kind of information about campaign finance online, there are great differences in the completeness of those releases and what formats are used to share them. Examining the current landscape of municipal campaign finance disclosure highlights opportunities for improvements, reveals the political levers that affect the openness of this data, and shows the kinds of accountability and context that can result from its release. With that noted, Idaho's statutes aim to protect political advertising transparency.

67-6613. **Commercial Reporting**. Each newspaper, periodical, broadcasting station, direct mailing company, printer and advertising agency which accepts expenditures from a political treasurer shall keep a current record (available to the public) listing the amounts paid and the obligations incurred by each candidate, political committee or political

> treasurer to such newspaper, periodical, broadcasting station, direct mailing company, printer or advertising agency.
> 67-6614A. **Publication or Distribution of Political Statements**. Whenever any person makes an expenditure for the purpose of financing communications expressly advocating the election, approval or defeat of a candidate, measure or person standing for election to the position of precinct committeeman through any broadcasting station, newspaper, magazine, outdoor advertising facility, direct mailing or any other type of general public political advertising, the person responsible for such communication shall be clearly indicated on such communication.

The layers of advertising law in Idaho will continue to evolve through court challenges, new services and products, and mediums used to connect with consumers. The law is a living entity with a willingness to adapt to protect consumers and attempt to keep advertising and marketing activities on level ground.

Advertising and marketing practices are not the enemy. It is important to remember that these practices have brought much good to the state, its people, and commerce. Nonetheless, there needs to be checks and balances to make a good thing better, and to keep the practice fair for all its participants.

References

Atwood, R (1985). Mass Communication Law in Idaho. Stillwater, OK: New Forums Press.

Joki, R. (2003). In the public interest: Idaho's communications law & issues handbook. Stillwater, OK: New Forums Press.

Linder, D (2016). Exploring Constitutional Law. Retrieved from http://law2.umkc.edu/faculty/projects/ftrials/conlaw/home.html

(2013). Adverising Law. Retrieved from https://www.hg.org/advert.html

(2016). Justia US Law. Retrieved from http://law.justia.com/idaho/

Chapter 7

Broadcast and Telecommunications Laws

By Katie Blevins, Ph.D.
Assistant Professor of Journalism, University of Idaho

The term "broadcast" traditionally refers to radio and television as mediums. The Federal Communications Commission (FCC) is an independent federal agency that takes on the role of regulating broadcast. The FCC was created by the Communications Act of 1934, for the purposes of "regulating interstate and foreign commerce in communication by wire and radio so as to make available, so far as possible, to all the people of the United States [...] Nation-wide, and world-wide wire and radio communications service" (The Media Bureau, 2008). The most important amendment of the Communications Act, the Telecommunications Act of 1996, addressed the internet, allowed for media cross-ownership, and attempted to open up the competitive market for telecommunications companies through deregulation. Based off these statutes, the federal government adopted the perspective of the "public interest, convenience, or necessity" (known as PICON), where the government regulated broadcast in "trust" for the public (47 U.S.C. §302(a), 307(d), 309(a) and 316(a)). These airwaves are maintained for public benefit and as a justification for federal intervention.

Broadcast is the least protected medium of speech, under the doctrine of medium specific jurisprudence. According to this doctrine, mediums are regulated differently due to a combination of historical and practical elements (*Joseph Burstyn, Inc. v. Wilson*, 1952). Historically, broadcast mediums were considered threatening to viewers. The perceived intrusiveness of radio and then television led to concerns about this new "technology." Justice John Paul Stevens, in the Supreme Court case *FCC v. Pacifica* (1978), which established broadcast as less protected than print, argued that:

> Of all forms of communication, broadcasting has the most limited First Amendment protection. Among the reasons for specially treating indecent broadcasting is the uniquely pervasive presence that medium of expression occupies in the lives of our people. Broadcasts extend into the privacy of the home, and it is impossible completely to avoid those that are patently offensive. Broadcasting, moreover, is uniquely accessible to children. (pp. 727-28).

Additionally, broadcast lacked the explicit protection provided for print and newspapers by the First Amendment's "free press" clause.

In terms of practical aspects, early case law focused on spectrum scarcity, where there were a limited number of frequencies available for channels. In *National Broadcasting Co. v. FCC* (1943), the United States Supreme Court for the first time used spectrum scarcity as a justification for regulating broadcast. The Court reinforced it as applicable for television in *Red Lion Broadcasting v. FCC* (1969).

Individual states do not take an active role in distributing radio or television licenses, determining signal strength, or regulating content. Instead the FCC examines whether any application to build a new station, modify or renew a station's license, or sell a station, serves the public's interest (The Media Bureau, 2008). Individual radio and television stations select the content they air, though the FCC regulates this content primarily for indecency. The FCC does not regulate internet content but *does* currently enforce a policy of net neutrality.

The FCC and Multiple Ownership Rules

The FCC attempts to preserve, in the spirit of the public's trust in the airwaves, a level of competition among radio and television stations by limiting cross ownership of radio, television and newspapers (justified by preserving multiple sources of local news). The FCC reassesses multiple ownership rules on a quadrennial basis, with the most recent report in August 2016 resolving outstanding issues with the 2010 and 2014 reviews.

Per the existing guidelines, in Boise for example: 1) a newspaper and broadcast station (AM, FM, or TV) cannot be owned by the same entity; 2) up to two local television stations can be owned by the same entity if the service areas do not overlap OR at least one station is not ranked in the top four of the Boise market AND eight independently owned stations remain in the market; 3) local radio and TV cross-ownership is allowed *if* a certain amount of independently owned "media voices" remain; 4) allowances for local radio cross-ownership is decided on a sliding scale- the larger the market with the larger number of stations allows for more cross-ownership by a single entity (FCC, 2015a).

The FCC and Net Neutrality

The internet's regulation status was in doubt until 1997, *Reno v. ACLU* (1997), when the Supreme Court ruled that the internet would be treated the same as print (historically the newspaper, book, and magazine industries). This distinction is important because under medium specific jurisprudence the internet is protected more than radio and television. As a result, there can be almost no regulation of internet *content*. The FCC does not regulate indecency, although other laws regulate all indecency. For example, under variable obscenity laws adult content that is legal for adults is considered obscene for children.

There remains some question in terms of regulating internet access. Many telecommunication companies distribute a combination of telephone, cellphone, cable television, satellite television, and internet service. Telecommunication companies are relatively centralized in the United States, resulting in most individuals only having one or two broadband companies to choose from (cable or telephone company that provides internet as well, some provide all three).

The United States has continued to allow for consolidation of many cable, television, internet, and media companies. In 2014, the FCC and Department of Justice were asked to review a possible merger between Comcast and Time Warner. This $45 billion deal would have followed on the heels of Comcast acquiring NBCUniversal in 2013, which gave Comcast control of a large amount of primetime television content via the NBC network. In the face of criticism over the merging of content and broadcast providers, as well as dwindling competition in telecommunications providers, the FCC and Department of Justice filed an antitrust lawsuit and the proposed merger was dropped in 2015 (Gelles, Ruiz, & Lipton, 2015).

The FCC has generally enforced a policy of net neutrality, where telecommunication companies that are internet service providers (ISPs), must treat all internet content the same. This means that there cannot be prioritization of content in terms of speed, user accessibility, etc. Although this has been the defacto standard, there have been a series of legal challenges regarding the FCC's authority to regulate net neutrality.

At the heart of this issue is the designation of ISPs as common carriers. Common carriers, or service-based companies- traditionally utility companies like gas, water, and telephone- must offer their services equally to all parties. Information or content-based services can refuse to do business with whomever they would like. The FCC has the authority to regulate common carriers in the context of broadcast, but cannot regulate non-common carriers.

The 2014 federal appellate case, *Verizon v. Federal Communications Commission* (2014), cast the ability of the FCC to enforce net neutrality into doubt. The U.S. Court of Appeals for the D.C. Circuit ruled that under the applicable definitions for common carriers in The Communications Act of 1934, broadband providers were not common carriers. Since the FCC can regulate common carriers but *not* non-common carriers, this essentially negated the ability of the FCC to enforce net neutrality.

The court did affirm the FCC's ability to push for nationwide broadband expansion as part of their mission of universal service and noted that The Communications Act of 1934 could be modified. In February 2015, the FCC passed new regulations that defined broadband providers as "telecommunications services," presumably defining them as common carriers. There will likely be legal challenges to this re-classification.

Telecommunication companies would prefer to move away from the standard of net neutrality. Especially as streaming content has grown in popularity and taken increased bandwidth, these companies argue that they would be able to provide cheaper access by tiering content - charging more for access to a streaming site like Netflix or YouTube. Speech advocates argue that the internet's "print" designation emphasizes the legal importance of maintaining net neutrality. In addition, the continued merging of telecommunication companies and content providers worries many observers.

State-Specific Telecommunication & Internet Regulation

The prominence of the FCC in telecommunications delegates state-specific regulation to very fragmented areas that intersect with federal requirements. This chapter will detail the places where state law addresses functional issues not covered by the FCC. Some of these regulations address telephone companies and are included as relevant under the modern conflation of telephone, broadband internet, cellular service, and smartphones.

Telecommunications Act of 1988

The Idaho legislature states that "universally available telecommunications services are essential to the health, welfare and economic well-being of the citizens of the state of Idaho and there is a need for establishing legislation to protect and maintain high-quality universal telecommunications at just and reasonable rates for all classes of customers and to encourage innovation within the industry by a balanced program of regulation and competition" (Telecommunications Act of 1988). To support these goals, the legislative intent is to: foster effective competition in the telecommunications market, examine the impact of deregulation and focus on the transition of the telecommunications industry from regulated public utility to competitive industry

This act was passed in 1988 and amended most recently in 1999. Very little of it appears on the surface to influence the modern understanding of telecommunications (ie: internet vs. telephone). That being said, the companies acting as internet service providers (ISPs) in Idaho are often telephone corporations, who provide internet via DSL, broadband, and mobile data (3G and 4G). Competition, universal access, and other broad regulations that limit or encourage these corporations directly affect the availability of *internet* in the state.

The Telecommunications Act of 1988 differentiates between telephone corporations as public utilities - "non-profit or cooperative telephone corporation" or "provide basic local exchange service"- and telephone corporations that fall outside this designation, which are considered telecommunications corporations. This is a somewhat different way of designating telephone corporations and is not clarified in light of the very recent FCC rulings on telecommunications companies, and whether they are common carriers/public utilities.

Under existing Idaho statute, despite some telephone corporations being regulated straight as public utilities-nonprofit, cooperative, or providing basic local exchange service - and some as subject to The Telecommunications Act of 1988, the description in both areas of state law seems to categorize them as common carriers. For example, under The Telecommunications Act of 1988 telephone corporations cannot have "any prejudice or competitive disadvantage with respect to its prices or charges for providing access to its local exchange network nor establish or maintain any unreasonable difference as to its prices or charges for access to its local exchange network." Enforcing equal treatment and access is the cornerstone of the federal definition of a common carrier. Applicable telephone companies are, under the Telecommunications Act of 1988, made to publically file their price lists, use averaged message service rates based off geographically similar companies, follow set requirements for subscriptions to local basic telephone service, and other cost-based concerns.

More relevant to the issue of telephone companies providing internet services, any telephone corporation subject to the law cannot withdraw or discontinue service unless there is "one or more alternative corporations [...] furnishing the respective telecommunication service or equivalent service to customers" (Telecommunications Act of 1988). Additionally, this statute preempts/prohibits any "economic, franchise or licensing regulation of telephone corporations subject to this law by cities, counties, incorporated or unincorporated areas, special use districts, or any other local governmental entity" (Telecommunications Act of 1988). This essentially recognizes the "open competition" concept stated in the legislative intent of the Telecommunications Act of 1988. It also puts the burden on the state in maintaining competition by disallowing local government regulation/licensing/profiting.

That being said, although the Idaho Telecommunications Act of 1988 was amended in direct response to the federal Telecommunications Act of 1996, in reality the effect of the Telecommunications Act of 1996 was widespread deregulation, a consolidation of telecommunications corporations, and a de-emphasis on competition in the marketplace (Telecommunications Act of 1996). Idaho statutes do not currently address these major shifts in the telecommunications landscape on the national level.

Universal Service

The Idaho Department of Health and Welfare distributes limited federal "lifeline" contributions to low-income residents to offset the cost of telecommunications services. These include nonprofit telephone companies and telecommunication corporations providing wireless, cellular, personal communication services, and mobile radio services. The legislative intent of this statute is to "promote universal service" to all Idaho residents (Idaho Code § 56-901).

Components of The Telecommunications Act of 1988 also address the goal of universal access from the telephone company's perspective. The statute establishes a universal service fund on a statewide level. The fund comes from a "statewide end user surcharge" on telephone lines, a "cents per line charge" that is collected by *all* telephone companies in the state, regardless of their regulatory designation. A commission distributes the funds back to telephone corporations who meet certain eligibility guidelines, with the goal of providing statewide telephone services to Idaho residents (Telecommunication Act of 1988).

Between these two aspects of universal access, the state tries to address gaps in telecommunications services both on an individual and corporate basis. This encourages better adoption rates overall as low-income residents in Idaho are compensated from federal funds and telephone corporations are compensated from state taxes.

Physical Provisions for Telecommunications Services

Several areas of state law address the physical requirements for telecommunications services. These telecommunications services—telephone and/or internet—often utilize "public rights-of-way," or the surface, air space, ground below, public streets, parks, waterways, to install access to these services. Under Idaho statute, telecommunications providers are subject to the relevant authority of cities, counties, or highway districts and do not have any property rights to these public rights-of-way (Idaho Code § 62-701).

In addressing the often-symbiotic nature between different telecommunications providers, Idaho Code addresses cable television providers and their rights to enter into agreements with public utilities who control telephone poles and/or ducts, or "rights-of-way," used in the installation of wired communication. Under this statute, the Idaho legislature recognizes "many public utilities have, through a course of conduct covering many years, made available space on and in their poles, ducts, conduits, and other support structures for use by the cable television industry for pole attachment service." Although public utilities can and do charge for this availability, if a public utility company and cable television company are unable to come to an agreement on "rates, terms or conditions" for access, the Idaho public utilities commission can step in and regulate to assure that the public utilities company recovers any additional cost generated from providing and maintaining pole attachments (Idaho Code § 61-538).

It is illegal for any individual to intentionally "prohibit, disrupt, inhibit, delay, disconnect or otherwise interfere" with a person's ability to contact emergency services by taking down or obstructing any telephone, electric, or wireless communications options. Emergency services include law enforcement, emergency medical services, fire department, etc. (Idaho Code § 18-6810).

Television Translator Stations

Television translator stations, also known as broadcast relay stations, simulcast licensed FCC channels, often to extend coverage of content to rural areas. The FCC does not maintain the same types of regulations on these translator stations (unless an owner is seeking an exception to a multiple ownership rule). They may be low-powered stations (LPTV), or full-power repeaters, and are indicated by call sign "K" west of the Mississippi, while full-power repeater stations often have "-TV" at the end of the call sign. Although true television stations regulated by the FCC had to switch from analog to digital signal in 2009 as a federal initiative, LPTV stations were given until September 2015 (FCC, 2015b). Full-powered repeaters were required to switch to digital broadcast by 2009 (FCC, 2011).

Since these television translator stations are not regulated the same by the FCC, state laws address their use and operation within Idaho. Television translator stations are defined as "any facility within this state which is operated to receive and amplify the signals broadcast by one or more television stations and redistribute the signals by appropriate broadcasting means but shall not include redistribution of signals by wire or cable" (Idaho Code § 31-4101). It is unclear what "appropriate broadcasting means" encompasses, but given the shift to digital broadcast, almost certainly digital stations fall within that scope. Excluded from this definition are community antenna systems, or cable TV, originally meant to distribute signals to rural communities (Idaho Code § 31-4102).

Prior to establishing a new translator district, a petition must be published in the relevant local newspaper(s) for three consecutive weeks with a notice about the plans for the district and the time of the local county commissioners meeting when the petition is discussed (Idaho Code § 31-4107). At the county commissioners meeting, the commissioners may either adopt or reject the plan for the new translator district. If they adopt it, the commissioners will also adopt a resolution detailing the specifics of that district (construction, location, type, cost, and how this will benefit the public's interest) as well as a board of trustees (Idaho Code § 31-4108, 4110).

Among the powers and duties outlined for these translator districts: "assure that there will be a fair, efficient, and equitable distribution of television services within the area," "acquire, build, construct, repair, own, maintain and operate any necessary stations transmitting simultaneous signals intended to be received by the general public, relay stations, pick-up stations, or any other electrical or electronic system necessary," and provide assessment rates for services rendered to the public, and apply for any federal/state permits or licenses (Idaho Code § 31-4114). These districts also have the right to enter into various contracts in the pursuit of their duties: make compensatory contracts to property owners whose property is being used, relevant government contracts such as a municipality, and lawful labor contracts with employees, engineers, attorneys, etc. (Idaho Code § 31-4114).

Television translator stations are supported by taxes from citizens within those districts. Citizens can receive an exemption from this tax if they receive the signal directly from the station the translator station is simulcasting from, do not receive the translator station signal into their home, or subscribe to cable television (Idaho Code § 31-4117). Fraudulent exemption claims from this tax are subject to a misdemeanor (Idaho Code § 31-4119).

Communications Security

It is illegal in the state of Idaho to possess, sell, advertise, give, or make illegal telecommunications equipment, defined as any device designed to steal telecommunications services (eg: cable television) or conceal activities. Other types of technology like clone/counterfeit cellular phones, which have altered electronic serial numbers so they are difficult to track, and related cloning paraphernalia are also illegal. Under this law, it is also illegal to possess, sell, advertise, give, or make plans for how to build these devices. Possession of these devices or plans to make these devices can result in criminal punishments as well as civil, where the impacted telecommunications company can sue (Idaho Code § 18-6713).

Additionally, it is a felony to intercept, ask another party to procure, willfully disclose, willfully use any "wire, electronic, or oral communication." There are significant exceptions made for interception of these communications as either an employee of a telecommunications company, operating within the scope of their hired duties, an agent of the FCC, or law enforcement operating under a warrant to intercept electronic communications (Idaho Code § 18-6702).

Although this statute falls within general federal guidelines, it does not address any exceptions for the publication of illegally gained information when the press legally gains access to it. The Supreme Court established this precedent in *New York Times Co. v. U.S.* (1971), when the New York Times legally published The Pentagon Papers, classified documents which were illegally leaked to them by Daniel Ellsberg, a U.S. military analyst. Justice William Brennan, in his concurrence of the per curiam opinion, notes that "So far as I can determine, never before has the United States sought to enjoin a newspaper from publishing information in its possession" (*New York Times Co. v. U.S.*, 1971, p. 725). Under this standard, as long as a news organization does not commit illegal activity to procure the content, they are free to publish it. Looking at this section of Idaho's Communications Secrecy law, it appears to suggest that any news organization willfully disclosing or using the contents of a "wire, electronic, or oral communication" could be subject to stiff criminal punishments, even if the news organization did not procure the information.

This issue has increased salience with the ease of data transfer. On the national stage, similar situations arose in 2010, when Private Chelsea Manning illegally leaked more than 700,000 classified files concerning ongoing conflicts in Iraq and Afghanistan, as well as diplomatic cables through the organization WikiLeaks (Savage & Huetteman, 2013). Although Manning served part of a 35-year prison sentence for leaking those files, news organizations published them without consequence. In 2013, CIA employee Edward Snowden released thousands of files concerning global and domestic surveillance programs run mostly by the National Security Agency (NSA) (Macaskill & Dance, 2013). He has stayed abroad to avoid prosecution while news organizations have disclosed and used this information without penalty.

Piracy

It is illegal under Idaho statute to transfer, sell, distribute, or advertised pirated content. This content is defined as "any sounds previously recorded on a phonograph record, disc, wire, tape, film or other article on which sounds are recorded with the intent to sell such articles, or cause them to be sold for profit or used to promote the sale of any product" not owned by the person in question (Tape Piracy Act, Idaho Code 18-76). There is a major exception for broadcasters though, who, in connection with the transmission of radio, television or cable television, can transfer sounds or audio recordings for archival purposes (Tape Piracy Act).

Public Schools and Libraries

It is a common practice to distribute federal or state funds for public schools and libraries based on the establishment of standards for internet use on their premises, or installing filters to block adult content. Internet standards are aimed at controlling the amount of adult content students and underage library patrons can access while using public resources.

The constitutionality of these types of regulations was established in the Supreme Court case, *United States v. American Library Association* (2003), which upheld the The Children's Internet Protection Act (2000). This federal statute requires K-12 schools and libraries receiving E-Rate discounts to install filters to continue to be eligible for federal funds.

In line with this, Idaho school districts must file an "acceptable internet use policy" with the state superintendent of public instruction. These policies must be resubmitted every five years. The legislative intent behind this statute is to "prevent the use of school computers [...] from sending, receiving, viewing or downloading materials that are deemed harmful to minors." Included in each policy is provisions for the selection of internet filters to facilitate in blocking access to "obscene materials, materials harmful to minors and materials that depict the sexual exploitation of a minor" (Idaho Code § 33-132).

Public libraries must also have a "policy of internet safety," which outlines how libraries will enforce technology measures to prevent minors using the library's computers for content that is obscene, child pornography, or harmful to minors. This technology most often takes the form of an internet filter.

Adults are legally allowed to access indecent content, which is considered harmful to minors, as a part of their First Amendment free speech rights. They do not have any right to access obscene content or child pornography, both of which are categories of unprotected speech. Therefore, adults can ask for filtering technology to be turned off any public library computer if they wish to access lawful content that the filter might block (*U.S. v. ALA*, 2003). Public library policies must be reviewed every three years by a library board of trustees, and be posted in a conspicuous place where library patrons can see it (Idaho Code § 33-2741).

Publication of Public Notices

Some public officials are required to publish certain notices required by law and may supplement that publication using radio and television (Idaho Code § 60-110). Broadcasters are required to keep a copy of a transcript of these broadcasts available to the public (Idaho Code § 60-111). In cases where proof of broadcast is required, an affidavit by the relevant station's manager, assistant manager, or program director with a transcript will suffice (Idaho Code § 60-112).

Liability

Under specific areas of Idaho law, broadcasters are exempt from liability. Specifically, radio and television broadcasters who participate in the voluntary broadcast notification system known as the "AMBER Alert," which notifies the public of missing or abducted children, are immune from civil liability (Idaho Code § 5-340).

Spam Emails

Many states have followed federal guidelines for targeting spam emails. The federal law, Controlling the Assault of Non-Solicited Pornography and Marketing (CAN-SPAM) Act of 2003, prohibits the use of false information in commercial emails and allows individuals to opt-out of subsequent messages from the same origin. Most states have passed similar legislation.

Under Idaho's Consumer Protection Act (1971), advertisers must "provide an electronic mail address readily identifiable in the bulk electronic mail advertisement to which the recipient may send a request for declining such mail." Commercial senders have five business days to process any opt-out requests from recipients. Aside from identification and opting out, commercial electronic mail senders must avoid use of a fictitious name, misrepresenting any information about the origin of the email, and not putting identifying information about the point of origin.

Recipients who receive any email that violates this statute may pursue civil action to recover actual damages-damages from any actual harm suffered from receiving the spam or junk email (monetary, emotional, etc.). Since this level of damages requires proof, the statute also provides recipients the option to receive a flat amount, $100 for each email received in violation of this statute or $1,000.

The combination of the FCC's influence and Idaho state laws addressed the state of broadcast and internet regulation for both companies and individuals seeking better understanding of telecommunications laws. Although these regulations and statutes vary, from ownership guidelines at the federal level to liability and library internet filters at the state level, taken as a whole they provide a comprehensive overview.

References (with unnamed Code)

47 U.S.C. §302(a), 307(d), 309(a) and 316(a).

CAN-SPAM Act, 15 U.S.C. §§ 7701-7713 (2004).

Consumer Protection Act, Idaho Code § 48-603.

FCC. (2011). *Rules for Digital LPTV, TV Translator, and Class A Television Stations*. Retrieved from https://www.fcc.gov/document/rules-digital-lptv-tv-translator-and-class-television-stations-0.

FCC. (2015a). *Consumer Guide: FCC's Review of Broadcast Ownership Rules*. Retrieved from http://transition.fcc.gov/cgb/consumerfacts/reviewrules.pdf.

FCC. (2015b). *DTV Transition and LPTV- Class A- Translator Stations*. Retrieved from https://www.fcc.gov/consumers/guides/dtv-transition-and-lptv-class-translator-stations.

Federal Communications Commission v. Pacifica Foundation, 438 U.S. 726 (1978).

Gelles, D., Ruiz, R., Lipton, E. (2015, April 23). Comcast is said to end $45 billion bid for Time Warner Cable. *The New York Times.* Retrieved from http://www.nytimes.com/2015/04/24/business/media/comcast-time-warner-cable-merger.html.

Idaho Code § 5-340.

Idaho Code § 18-6702, 13.

Idaho Code § 18-6810.

Idaho Code § 31-4101-2, 7-8, 10, 14, 17, 19.

Idaho Code § 33-132.

Idaho Code § 33-2741.

Idaho Code § 56-901.

Idaho Code § 60-110-112.

Idaho Code § 61-538.

Idaho Code § 62-701.

Joseph Burstyn, Inc. v. Wilson, 343 U.S. 495, 503, (1952).

Macaskill, E. & Dance, G. (2013, Nov. 1). NSA files: Decoded. *The Guardian.* Retrieved https://www.theguardian.com/world/interactive/2013/nov/01/snowden-nsa-files-surveillance-revelations-decoded#section/1.

National Broadcasting Co. v. FCC, 319 U.S. 190 (1943).

New York Times Co. v. U.S., 403 U.S. 713 (1971).

Red Lion Broadcasting v. FCC, 395 U.S. 367 (1969).

Reno v. American Civil Liberties Union, 521 U.S. 844 (1997).

Savage, C. & Huetteman, E. (2013, Aug. 21). Manning sentenced to 35 years for pivotal leak of

U.S. files. *The New York Times.* Retrieved http://www.nytimes.com/2013/08/22/us/manning-sentenced-for-leaking-government-secrets.html.

Tape Piracy Act, Idaho Code §18-7603, 06.

Telecommunications Act of 1988, Idaho Code § 62-602, 604, 606-612, 618.

Telecommunications Act of 1996, Pub. L. No. 104-104, § 110, 56 Stat. (1996).

The Media Bureau. (2008). How to get the most from your service location. *The Public and*

Broadcasting (FCC Publication). Retrieved from https://www.fcc.gov/media/radio/public-and-broadcasting.

United States v. American Library Association, 539 U.S. 194 (2003).

Verizon v. FCC, 740 F.3d 623 (D.C. Cir. 2014).

Chapter 8

Newsroom Searches and Court Access by Media

By Katie Blevins, Ph.D.
Assistant Professor of Journalism, University of Idaho

Rebecca Tallent, Ed.D.
Associate Professor of Journalism, University of Idaho

There are many areas of law that explicitly involve media interests. This chapter draws on two more auxiliary areas of legal concern involving access to information: What rights law enforcement has to conduct searches of newsrooms for information and what rights individuals have to attend courtrooms. The law regarding how *journalists* can collect information is fairly clear and is addressed under areas of law like fraud, trespass and surveillance/recording. The law regarding government meetings is limited to federal executive agencies (and state executive agencies), and governed by federal and state transparency law.

These auxiliary areas of newsroom searches and courtroom access fill in where the more clearly distinct areas of law do not extend. While there is some Idaho-specific state law that touches on newsroom searches and courtroom access, these areas are largely defined by a mix of case law, federal statutes, and state statutes.

Law Enforcement and Newsroom Searches

The first prominent legal attempt to address newsroom searches was a U.S. Supreme Court case, *Zurcher v. Stanford Daily* (1978). In *Zurcher* (1978), a student newspaper which had published photographs and articles about a clash between demonstrators and the police at a hospital, brought action against several groups, including the police department and the office of the district attorney. The newspaper claimed a search warrant was issued by a local judge under probable cause that the newspaper staff had information about the names of the demonstrators who had attacked the police. The warrant covered student files on the stories, photographs and negatives taken at the event; the respondents claimed they had been denied their constitutional rights, especially under the Fourth Amendment.

The District Court ruled the Fourth Amendment, as made applicable to the states by the Fourteenth Amendment, forbids the issuance of a warrant to search for materials relating to a crime if the person in question is not part of the crime unless there is probable cause (based on facts in a sworn affidavit) to believe a subpoena would be impracticable. The court also said it would need to appear the person holding the information would not destroy or remove the data. Finally, the court said the newspaper was an innocent object of the search, but the First Amendment makes the search constitutionally permissible. The U.S. Supreme Court affirmed the Ninth Circuit's decision, but established stricter standards for newsroom searches.

In writing the majority opinion, Justice Byron White (1978) said:

> The right of the people to be secure in their persons, houses, papers, and effects, against unreasonable searches and seizures, shall not be violated, and no Warrants shall issue, but upon probable cause, supported by Oath or affirmation, and particularly describing the place to be searched, and the persons or things to be seized.
>
> ... Aware of the long struggle between Crown and press and desiring to curb unjustified official intrusions, the Framers took the enormously important step of subjecting searches to the test of reasonableness and to the general rule requiring search warrants issued by neutral magistrates. They nevertheless did not forbid warrants where the press was involved, did not require special showings that subpoenas would be impractical, and did not insist that the owner of the place to be searched, if connected with the press, must be shown to be implicated in the offense being investigated. Further, the prior cases do no more than insist that the courts apply the warrant requirements with particular exactitude when First Amendment interests would be endangered by the search. As we see it, no more than this is required where the warrant requested is for the seizure of criminal evidence reasonably believed to be on the premises occupied by a newspaper. Properly administered, the preconditions for a warrant -- probable cause, specificity with respect to the place to be searched and the things to be seized, and overall reasonableness -- should afford sufficient protection against the harms that are assertedly threatened by warrants for searching newspaper offices.

This Supreme Court case established that while the specifics of The Stanford Daily meant there was probable cause and the "third party" search did not violate the paper's Fourth Amendments rights, such searches *did* require warrants and probable cause that the newsroom search was necessary to upholding the law.

Partially in reaction to *Zurcher* (1978), Congress passed The Privacy Protection Act (1980) to provide stronger protections for journalists. This statute established the federal standard that newsroom searches are presumptively illegal and require a subpoena to be legal. Part of the purpose of this statute is to limit "fishing" by law enforcement, where officials might suspect journalists have information tangential to open investigations. Searching the newsroom just to gather, or "fish" for information, is illegal. Under this act, the government can only conduct searches of newsrooms if the journalist is suspected of committing the crime themselves, or if there is a direct threat of death or bodily harm and the seized information will remedy that threat.

The Idaho State Constitution, Article 1 Section 17, does not extend any additional protections to the federal statute. It only outlines, non-specific to newsrooms, that the peoples right to be "secure in their persons, houses, papers and effects against unreasonable searches and seizures shall not be violated; and no warrant shall issue without probable cause shown by affidavit, particularly describing the place to be searched and the person or thing to be seized."

There is some concern two additional federal statutes might provide an avenue of exemption to the protections that The Privacy Protection Act (1980) put in place. Specifically, these are The Foreign Intelligence Surveillance Act (FISA), passed in 1978, and significantly strengthened by the USA PATRIOT Act (2001), in the aftermath of 9/11. Under the FISA, a secret spy court was created that allowed FISA judges to issue secret warrants authorizing domestic wiretaps and searches. The FISA court operates outside the traditional transparency requirements of most federal courts, citing national security as a reason for secrecy. The powers of the FISA court were augmented by the USA PATRIOT Act in 2001, which allows government officials to seize materials from businesses (newsrooms included), related to foreign intelligence information. Businesses, or newsrooms, subject to FISA warrants are automatically placed under a gag order, keeping them from revealing that a search and seizure was ever conducted. The secret nature of the FISA court makes it difficult to gauge its impact on newsrooms.

Idaho Criminal Rule 41allows a judge or magistrate to issue a search and seizure warrant on behalf of any law enforcement officer or attorney in the state. Specifically, Rule 41 (2013) states:

> (b) Property or person which may be seized with a warrant. A warrant may be issued under this rule to search for and seize
>
> (1) evidence of the commission of a criminal offense; or
> (2) contraband, the fruits of crime, or things otherwise criminally possessed; or
> (3) weapons or other things by means of which a crime has been committed or reasonably appears about to be committed; or
> (4) a person named in an arrest warrant issued pursuant to Rule 4 of these rules.

There is no exception allowed for the news media. The Reporter's Committee for Freedom of the Press (n.d.) states:

> The federal Privacy Protection Act (42 U.S.C. 2000aa) has not been implicated in any reported Idaho decisions. Given the hostility of the Idaho Supreme Court to the reporter's privilege generally, and its specific endorsement of the rul-

ing in *Stanford Daily v. Zurcher*, 436 U.S. 547 (1978) (the case which gave rise to the passage of the Privacy Protection Act) in the *Caldero* case, it is unlikely that there would be any protection against newsroom searches in Idaho but for the protections afforded under the Privacy Protection Act. There are no similar state statutes.

Most questions about searching videotape go back to *Citicasters v. McCaskill*, a 1996 case out of Kansas City, Missouri. In this case, WDAF-TV recorded evidence of an abduction which concluded with a murder. The video was taken of the abduction by a tourist and sold to WDAF. Kansas City law enforcement requested and received a search warrant to obtain the videotape, the station objected. In the lawsuit, the TV station claimed Jackson County, Missouri, prosecutor Claire C. McCaskill and the local police department had violated the Privacy Protection Act of 1980 in seizing the videotape from the TV station. McCaskill appealed, saying the district court erred in barring her from showing the circumstances exempted her from The Privacy Act. The appeals court agreed with McCaskill and remanded the case back to the lower court, although the lower court denied the request for rehearing in 1997. The impact of this case is in some of the legal discussion the Eight Circuit Court of Appeals ruled the constitutionality of The Privacy Act (1980), could be called into question. Although as of now, the act remains intact and unchallenged.

The lack of reporter's privilege in Idaho can at times result in case law that looks at related but unaddressed areas like newsroom access. In 1996, the Supreme Court of Idaho ruled on a case, *State v. Salsbury*, involving the subpoena of a videotape taken by a reporter for KMVT at the scene of a fatal car accident. A newspaper reporter for The Twin Falls Times-News, Michael J. Salsbury, was arrested at the scene of the accident and was charged with resisting and obstructing a police officer. The KMVT news crew got parts of the incident involving Salsbury on tape while covering the accident. Law enforcement later subpoenaed the videotape as evidence against Salsbury.

The Idaho Supreme Court ruled the videotape was a "public event which was readily viewable to anyone present." The public nature of the event, despite the fact that it was captured on videotape only by the KMVT news crew, essentially meant there would be no chilling effect on journalists involved by forcing the television station to comply with the subpoena. This was a balancing of the federal standard set for reporter's privilege in the Supreme Court case *Branzburg v. Hayes* (1972).

Courtroom Access

Freedom of Information laws are a body of laws on the federal and state level that guarantee a measure of government transparency with regards to federal and state level executive agencies. These laws do not cover access to other branches of government, such as the courts. In *Richmond v. Virginia* (1980), the Supreme Court addressed the question of whether or not criminal trials can be closed to the public and the press.

In this case, a series of mistrials for a murder case in the state of Virginia were closed to both the public at large as well as the media by the trial judge. Two reporters for Richmond Newspapers challenged this closure, citing it violated their First Amendment rights.

The Supreme Court ruled there is an "implicit" First Amendment right for people to attend a criminal trial. Although "public trials" are not expressly outlined by the First Amendment, the intent of the First Amendment is to protect not just freedom of speech, expression, and the press, but also the ability to receive certain information. In the Supreme Court opinion, Chief Justice Warren E. Burger noted "historical evidence of the evolution of the criminal trial in Anglo-American justice demonstrates conclusively that, at the time this Nation's organic laws were adopted, criminal trials both here and in England had long been presumptively open" (*Richmond v. Virginia*, 1980, p. 556). Additionally, the First Amendment explicitly guarantees a right to assembly and courtrooms are places where the public has traditionally gathered.

The *appearance* of justice is almost as important as the justice itself (*Richmond v. Virginia*, 1980, 556). In other words, the judicial process must have a level of transparency guaranteed so individuals can see it working and trust in the system. This is especially true in criminal trials, where the result of the government winning a court case is jail time.

This extension of the First Amendment, beyond its written text, is known as penumbral reasoning. A "penumbra" is a "space of partial illumination between the perfect shadow … on all sides and the full light" (Penumbra, 2003). In legal applications, a court will extend the shadow of certain constitutional rights by recognizing an *implicit* right. This first originated in a court case in 1871, *Montgomery v. Bevans*, and defined by Supreme Court Justice Oliver Holmes as the "gray area where logic and principles falter" (Holmes, 1873). For example, it has been used by the Supreme Court to justify a constitutional right to privacy, despite the word privacy not existing anywhere in the Constitution (*Griswold v. Connecticut*, 1965). Although there are no Supreme Court cases which extended openness to civil trials, most civil trials are open to the public.

Other aspects of courtroom access were addressed by two subsequent Supreme Court cases: *Press-Enterprise Co. v. Superior Ct.* (1984), and *Press-Enterprise Co. v. Superior Ct.* (1986), known subsequently as *Press-Enterprise I and Press-Enterprise II.* Both cases involved challenges made by The Press-Enterprise, a daily newspaper in Southern California, against courts in California. In *Press-Enterprise I* (1984), the Idaho Supreme Court affirmed the public and press had the right to attend not just the criminal trial itself, but also the jury selection process. In *Press-Enterprise II* (1986), the Supreme Court affirmed the public and press had the right to also attend pretrial and preliminary hearings for criminal trials.

While controversial as an approach to constitutional interpretation, a Supreme Court's interpretation of the Constitution is binding on lower courts and the states. So, the Court's decision to grant access to criminal trials had the wide-sweeping effect of requiring all future criminal trials to be open to the public at both the federal and state level. The United States Supreme Court does acknowledge there are instances where a criminal trial can be closed to the public and press, but it requires an "overriding interest articulated in findings" (Richmond v. Virginia, 581).

Specific to Idaho, the Idaho state constitution, approved in 1890, clearly articulates open trials as a defacto standard in Article I, Section 18: "JUSTICE TO BE FREELY AND SPEEDILY ADMINISTERED. Courts of justice shall be open to every person, and a speedy remedy afforded for every injury of person, property or character, and right and justice shall be administered without sale, denial, delay, or prejudice." This falls in line with the subsequent Supreme Court opinions outlined above.

In 1990, there was a case heard by the Supreme Court

of Idaho, *Cowles Publishing v. Frazier*, which looked at applying the precedent laid out by the Supreme Court's *Press-Enterprise II* (1986). In this case, Joshua Frazier was charged with first degree murder, possession of a deadly weapon and conspiracy to commit aggravated assault in Kootenai County; Frazier's attorney petitioned the court for a closed hearing. Cowles Publishing, also known as The Spokesman Review, argued seeking public access to the hearing, which was denied. The appeals court cited the *Press-Enterprise II* case upholding the First Amendment right of the press and public to preliminary hearings, that the hearings cannot be closed unless there are specific findings which show the defendant will not be able to get a fair trial due to pre-trial publicity. In the ruling, the court concluded: "As this court looks at it, the present state of the Idaho law does not keep secret the preliminary hearing proceedings, but delays the release of such information in certain cases where the defendant demands closure until the defendant is placed on trial or pleads guilty. The prosecution seldom benefits from a preliminary hearing. It is primarily for the benefit of the defense to test the state's case (*Cowles Publishing v. Frazier*, 1990)."

Exceptions to Courtroom Access

There are certain situations where both criminal and civil trials may be closed to the public and the press. These are general exceptions to courtroom access and are guidelines, based on federal and state standards. There may be special circumstances that impact public and press access to a trial.

The balance between the First Amendment rights of the press and public to receive information, must be balanced with the Sixth Amendment rights of the defendants in a criminal trial. Of particular concern is guaranteeing an impartial jury in a prominent trial with a significant amount of pretrial publicity. In situations where the freedom of the press/public unduly jeopardizes the fair trial rights of a defendant, courts have been able to take a variety of actions, from banning media reporting on the trial to putting a gag order on individuals participating in the trial to keep them from talking to the press. The Supreme Court addressed when a judge can issue a gag order in a 1976 court case, *Nebraska Press Association v. Stuart*.

States are also allowed to adopt rules governing the use of technology in the courtroom. This ranges from cameras, recording proceedings, to the use of cellphones, social media, etc. In Idaho, there is an Idaho Court Administrative Rule allowing cameras and recording equipment in the courtroom. The basic premise of this rule is there can be "audio/visual coverage" in the courtroom with advance permission from the presiding judge. This coverage is defined as "broadcast, video, audio, and photographic coverage or recording of public proceedings before district and magistrate judges. Broadcast means the transmission of images or sounds by any electronic means, including but not limited to television, radio, Internet, email or streaming" (I.C.A.R. 45-a).

That being said, the judge retains the right to revoke the use of this technology at any time without any prior notice. There are also very specific limitations on limiting the number of "still photographers" and "video and broadcast camera operator[s]" to one, and requiring media representatives to pool resources. Additionally, there are limitations on the use of this technology (essentially no disruptions of the court), and prohibiting coverage of certain aspects of a trial like photographing or taping the jury.

Idaho Court Administrative Rule 49-a specifically addresses electronic devices in court facilities, defining these devices as "cell phones, personal computers, personal digital assistants, and other similar devices capable of transmitting, receiving, recording or storing messages, images, sounds, data or other information by electronic means." These devices can be used in the courtroom for note taking and those notes can be transmitted while in the courtroom or court facility. Recording and transmission of court proceedings cannot violate the guidelines set by Administrative Rule 45, though. Violating any aspect of this Rule may result in being held in contempt of court.

Certain types of evidence (in the form of exhibits), may not be accessible to the public and press. Under the Idaho Court Administrative Rule 32-d-9, the "public shall not have access at any time to items of contraband or items that pose a health or safety hazard; for example, drugs, weapons, child pornography, toxic substances, or bodily fluids, without permission of the custodian judge."

Additionally, most court proceedings may be closed to the public and press if they involve juveniles. This a widespread exemption to courtroom access, given the sensitive nature of under-aged defendants. This is addressed both in terms of juvenile court records, ICAR 32-9, as well as any court proceedings, Idaho Juvenile Rule 52.

References

Cameras In the Courtroom, 45 ICAR (2010).

Citicasters v. McCaskill, 89 F.3d 1350 (1996).

Closed Hearings, 52 IJR (2006).

Cowles Publishing v. Frazier, 118 Idaho 753 (1990).

Electronic Devices in Court Facilities, 49 ICAR (2013).

Griswold v. Connecticut, 381 U.S. 479 (1965).

Holmes, O.W. (1873). The theory of torts. *American Law Review, 7*, 652.

Idaho Const. art. I, § 17.

Idaho Const. art. I, § 18.

Idaho Criminal Rule 41 (2013). Search and seizure. Retrieved on Feb. 2, 1017 from https://isc.idaho.gov/icr41

Idaho Juvenile Rule 52. Closed hearings (C.P.A.) (J.C.A.) Idaho Supreme Court. Retrieved from https://isc.idaho.gov/ijr52

Kristensen, D. (2010). Newsroom searches. In *Idaho-Privilege Compendium* (IX). Retrieved from http://www.rcfp.org/idaho-privilege-compendium/newsroom-searches.

Montgomery v. Bevans, 17 F. Cas. 628 (9th C.C.D. Cal.) (1871).

Merriam-Webster's collegiate dictionary (11th ed.). (2003). Penumbra. Springfield, MA: Merriam-Webster.

Nebraska Press Association v. Stuart, 427 U.S. 539 (1976).

Press-Enterprise Co. v. Superior Ct. 464 U.S. 501 (1984).

Press-Enterprise Co. v. Superior Ct. 478 U.S. 1 (1986).

Privacy Protection Act, 42 U.S.C. §2000aa et seq.

RCFP. (2011). Newsroom searches—FISA warrants. In *The First Amendment Handbook* (4). Retrieved from https://www.rcfp.org/first-amendment-handbook/newsroom-searches-fisa-warrants.

Records of The Judicial Department - Examination and Copying - Exemption From and Limitations on Disclosure, 32 ICAR (2016).

Richmond Newspapers v. Virginia, 448 U.S. 555 (1980).

Search and Seizure, 41 ICR (2013).

State v. Salsbury, 924 P.2d 208, 213-14 (Idaho 1996).

Zurcher v. Stanford Daily, 436 U.S. 547 (1978).

Chapter 9

Commercial Speech and Advertising

By Shaakirrah R. Sanders
Associate Professor of Law, University of Idaho

The Idaho Supreme Court has not directly addressed commercial speech and advertising as it relates to the media. The First Amendment[1] limits regulations and rules as they relate to commercial speech and advertising. In 1976 in *Virginia State Board of Pharmacy v. Virginia Citizens Consumer Council, Inc.*,[2] the U.S. Supreme Court struck down a law that punished licensed pharmacists for publishing, advertising, or promoting any price, fee, premium, discount, rebate, or credit term for prescription drugs.[3] Virginia argued the law was necessary to maintain professionalism.[4] The Court held that the constitutional elements of the pharmacist's speech remained even where "money was spent to project" that speech.[5] Moreover, advertisements were part of the free flow of commercial information that is of interest to the consumer and the public.[6] This holds true even where an advertiser's interest was purely economic.[7] The First Amendment does allow regulation to combat false, deceptive, misleading, or illegal speech, but such regulations cannot prohibit protected speech.[8] On this point, the Court held that Virginia's advertising ban was too broad to justify the state's interest in combatting unprofessionalism.[9]

Virginia State Board of Pharmacy demonstrates that in the commercial realm, false speech—even that of the media—is not protected for its own sake. Neither is deceptive or misleading speech.[10] Justice Rehnquist, who dissented in that case, warned against opening "the door to active promotion of prescription drugs, liquor, cigarettes, and other products whose usage the state deems desirable to discourage."[11] Perhaps in response to Justine Rehnquist's concerns, the Court established a standard for commercial speech regulations in *Central Hudson Gas & Electric Corp. v. Public Service Commission of New York*.[12] *Central Hudson* involved an advertising ban imposed by the Public Service Commission of New York against electric utilities in the state.[13] The Commission had previously determined that New York lacked sufficient fuel stocks or sources of supply to meet consumer demands for the winter of 1973-74.[14] Three years later the Commission continued the ban even though the fuel shortage had abated.[15] Justice Powell wrote for the majority and established that commercial speech regulations must be proportional to the state's interest.[16]

Central Hudson did not involve commercial speech regulations against the media, but in that case the Court does set the standard for commercial speech regulations and could apply to media promotions and advertisement. The Court established that the state's interests must be substantial and that limitations on expression must be carefully designed to directly advance the state's substantial interest.[17] This means that limitations cannot be remote, ineffective or only indirectly advance the state's interest.[18] Limitations must also constitute the least restrictive alternative for achieving the state's goal.[19] The state's interest cannot be served by a less severe restriction and must be narrowly drawn.[20] The state has the burden to make this showing, which requires proof of the following:

a. Whether the speech advertised illegal or unlawful activities or was false or deceptive.[21]
b. Whether the law was justified by a substantial interest.[22]
c. Whether the law directly advanced the state's interest.[23]
d. Whether the law was no more extensive than necessary.[24]

Central Hudson does not does address the standard that applies when media speech is punished for its *effect* on commerce or other economic interests. The latter category of speech has a long history and often involves "the use of deception, misrepresentation, and other practices associated with undercover investigation to uncover or observe facts and practices otherwise obscured from public view."[25] For example, in the 1890s Nellie Bly went undercover to write about conditions in mental institutions.[26] Upton Sinclair wrote about working conditions in the meatpacking industry after going undercover for seven weeks at meatpacking plants in Chicago's stockyards.[27] Sinclair's expose was the catalyst for an investigation by President Theodore Roosevelt that ultimately led to the Meat Inspection Act and the Pure Food and Drug Act in 1906.[28] Secret filming and photographs in the 1950s, 1960s, and 1970s were "used to document ... the operations of bookie parlors in St. Louis"[29] and the brutal response to the peaceful resistance of the Jim Crow south and the Vietnam War.[30] One undercover reporter in the 1970s, William Sherman of the *New York Daily News*, actually "won a Pulitzer Prize for reporting conducted while posing as a patient to expose Medicaid fraud."[31] More recently, police shootings captured on cell phone video have renewed public debate on racial profiling and the use of force by law enforcement.

The necessity for jurisprudence on liability for media speech that has a negative commercial effect may seem remote. However, the United States Supreme could be asked to address the issue as it relates to recent legislative measures in Idaho to insulate agriculture and animal farms and facilities from citizens, reporters, employees, and whistleblowers.[32] Food journalist Mark Bittman coined the term "ag-gag" to describe such legislation.[33] Loosely defined, ag-gag legislation is that which aims to prevent the release of damaging information from inside an agriculture or animal facility. Ag-gag legislation restricts—or "gags"—speech to the public about the conditions of food production.

Idaho is not the only state with a statute that aims to shield the agriculture industry from media scrutiny; such legislation also exists in **Iowa**,[34] **Kansas**,[35] **Missouri**,[36] **Montana**,[37] **North Carolina**,[38] **North Dakota**,[39] **Utah**,[40] **and Wyoming**.[41] Idaho's ag-gag legislation falls into three of the four broad categories of similar legislation.[42] Idaho criminalized obtaining and releasing information about food production activities. Idaho also criminalized lying to owners of agriculture facilities about employment motives. Finally, Idaho imposed civil liability for the release of information that reflects poorly on an animal or agriculture facility. Idaho did not impose a reporting requirement for information about animal abuse.

So far, Amy Meyers, a Utah resident, has been the only person charged under an ag-gag law.[43] Meyers drove to the Dale Smith Meatpacking Company in Draper City, Utah and from the side of the road video-recorded cows through a barbed-wire fence.[44] The recording depicted "[a] live cow who appeared to be sick or injured being carried away from the building in a tractor . . . as though she were nothing more than rubble."[45] An employee at Dale Smith Meatpacking Company tried to stop the filming, but Meyer replied that she was had the right to film because she was on a public easement.[46] Law enforcement arrived to investigate the employee's trespass complaint.[47] The police report noted "there was no damage to the fence."[48] Meyer was later charged with violating Utah's ag-gag law.[49] The charges were ultimately dismissed, but Meyer reported that the experience had a "chilling effect" on her ability to gather and disseminate the news.[50]

Idaho is the only state to have had its ag-gag statute ruled unconstitutional. *Animal Legal Defense Fund v. Otter*[51] involved a challenge to Idaho Code § 18-7042, which was entitled "interference with agricultural production."[52] Punishment for violation of section 18-7042 ranged to up to one year in jail and damages of up to twice the economic loss to a business.[53] During the legislative debate over section 18-7042, some of Idaho's legislators described animal rights investigators and activists as marauding invaders, terrorists, enemies to be combated, hostage takers, and extreme activists.[54] Others in Idaho's legislature also expressed a desire to shield Idaho dairymen and other farmers from undercover investigations and whistleblowers who expose the agricultural industry to the court of public opinion.[55] Still other legislators expressed concern for misrepresented, fraudulent, and defamatory editing of videos about agricultural operatons.[56]

In August 2015, the Honorable B. Lynn Winmill, Chief Judge of the United States District Court for the District of Idaho, ruled that section 18-7042 violated the First Amendment's freedom of speech and press clauses, as well as the Fourteenth Amendment's guarantee of equal protection.[57] Winmill likened section 18-7042 to Sinclair's *The Jungle*,[58] and held that the 1906 classic provides a clear illustration of how Section 18-7042 implicates the First Amendment.[59] Winmill theorized that Sinclair would face criminal punishment and restitution for the publication of his novel.[60] Winmill rejected Idaho's argument that section 18-7042 was designed to only protect private property.[61] According to Winmill, agricultural operations are not exclusively a private matter[62] and food production was a heavily regulated industry.[63]

Winmill had previously ruled on a pre-trial motion that section 18-7042 was a content-based restriction on speech, thus the highest level of scrutiny applied.[64] In performing this analysis, Winmill reasoned that section 18-7042 was too broad and could apply beyond fraud, defamation, conversion, or trespass.[65] The most likely harm from activity in violation of section 18-7042 would be the reporting on the facility itself, not reports about the representations made to gain access to that facility.[66] But, section 18-7042 applied even where only truthful activities were revealed.[67] Generally, harm caused by true stories is not a type of legally cognizable harm under the First Amendment.[68] Moreover, section 18-7042 only targeted speech concerning the conduct of an agricultural production facilitie's operations while activity, speech, and conduct regarding other facilities was left unburdened.[69] Section 18-7042 also only imposed damages if the prohibited activity reflected negatively upon the agriculture or animal facility.[70] Judge Winmill ultimately found that section 18-7042's underlying purpose was to suppress particular ideas, which the First Amendment prohibits.[71] On this point, Winmill noted that violators of section 18-7042 faced double the jail time than that of animal abusers and that violators of section 18-7042 were liable for double economic losses suffered by their "victims."[72]

Winmill's decision striking down Idaho's ag-gag law is currently pending appeal in the Ninth Circuit.[73] Federal litigation challenging North Carolina and Utah's ag-gag statutes remains in the pre-trial stage. However, a federal court upheld Wyoming's ag-gag statute, which is somewhat different from Idaho's statute.[74] Wyoming "prohibited collection of 'resource data' on 'open lands' without express permission or authorization." [75] The statute originally applied to both public and private land, but the Wyoming legislature amended the statute to only apply on private land.[76] Scott Skavdahl, United States District Judge for the District of Wyoming, ruled that there was no right to trespass on private property, and that trespassers and uninvited guests have no right exercise speech rights on private property.[77] Skavdahl found no evidence of animus towards environmental groups or other particular interest groups or viewpoints, despite evidence in the legislative record of comments negatively targeting such groups.[78] Those comments were contained in the legislative record of Wyoming's original ag-gag statute and were thus "cured" by the subsequently amended statute.[79] Skavdahl did not rule on whether Wyoming's ag-gag statute restricted speech on matters within the public's interest.

Should the constitutionality of an ag-gag statute reach the United States Supreme Court, the extent of First Amendment protection for undercover investigations, as well as the tools by which individuals seek to discover that information, could likely be addressed.[80] As discussed by Professor Brooke Kroeger, deceptive techniques "are critical to American journalism, and in particular to journalism involving conditions and practices in agricultural production facilities."[81] The Court may also consider how misrepresentations are already actionable under tort law and existing criminal codes. This could lead the Court to further ponder the effect of alleged media misrepresentations or other types of false speech as it relates to commercial activity.

Endnotes

1 U.S. CONST. amend. I.

2 425 U.S. 748 (1976).

3 *Vir. State Bd. of Pharmacy*, 425 U.S. at 750-52.

4 *Id.* at 752.

5 *Id.* at 761.

6 *Id.* at 755-56; 763-66; 769-70.

7 *Id.* at 762-63.

8 *Id.* at 772.

9 *Id.*

10 *Id.* at 771.

11 *Id.* at 781 (Rehnquist, J. dissenting).

12 447 U.S. 557 (1980).

13 *Central Hudson Gas & Electric Corp.*, 447 U.S. at 559-61.

14 *Id.* at 558-59.

15 *Id.* at 559.

16 *Id.* at 558, 564-66.

17 *Id.* at 564.

18 *Id.*

19 *Id.*

20 *Id.*

21 *Id.* at 566.

22 *Id.*

23 *Id.*

24 *Id.*

25 *See* Brief of Amici Curiae Professors Brooke Kroeger and Ted Conover in Support of Affirmance, p. 5, No. 15-35960, Animal Legal Defense Fund v. Wasden (9th Cir. 2016).

26 Diane Leenheer Zimmerman, *I Spy: The Newsgatherer Under Cover*, 33 U. Rich. L. Rev. 1185, 1190 (2000).

27 *See* UPTON SINCLAIR, THE JUNGLE (1906).

28 Animal Legal Defense Fund v. Otter, 118 F.Supp.3d 1195, 1202 (D. Idaho Aug. 3, 2015).

29 James H. Dygert, *The Investigative Journalist: Folk Heroes of a New Era VIII* (1976).

30 Brief for Amici Curiae Abrams Institute for Freedom of Expression and Scholars of First Amendment and Information Law in Support of Appellees, p. 5-8, No. 15-35960, Animal Legal Defense Fund v. Wasden (9th Cir. 2016).

31 *See Zimmerman*, *supra* note 26, at 1190 n.21.

32 Idaho Code 18-7042 (prohibiting interference with agricultural production), *overturned* by Animal Legal Defense Fund v. Otter, 118 F.Supp.3d 1195 (D. Idaho. 2016).

33 Mark Bittman, "Who Protects the Animals?," *The New York Times*, April 26, 2011 *available at* http://opinionator.blogs.nytimes.com/2011/04/26/who-protects-the-animals/?_r=0.

34 Iowa Code 717A.2 (criminalizing providing false information on an employment application at an agricultural facility with an intent to record images).

35 K.S.A. 47-1825-1830 (criminalizing "entering an animal facility to take pictures by photograph, video camera or by any other means" with the intent of causing harm to the enterprise).

36 Missouri Rev. Stat. 578.013.1 (imposing duty to submit recordings of alleged farm animal abuse within 24 hours of recording).

37 Montana Code 81-30-101 (criminalizing entering an animal facility with the intent to record images or take pictures for purposes of criminal defamation and criminalizing failing to report evidence of cruelty to animals within 24 hours).

38 N.C. Gen. Stat. 99A-2.

39 N. Dakota Cen. Code 12.1-21.1 (prohibiting entering "an animal facility and using or attempting to use a camera, video recorder, or any other

video or audio recording equipment").

40 Utah Code 76-6-112 (criminalizing providing false information on an employment application with the intent to record images at a farm).

41 Wyoming Code 6-3-414 (prohibiting trespassing to unlawfully collect resource data).

42 Idaho Code 18-7042.

43 Will Potter, *First "Ag-Gag" Prosecution: Utah Woman Filmed a Slaughterhouse from the Public Street*, available at: http://www.greenisthenewred.com/blog/first-ag-gag-arrest-utah-amy-meyer/6948/.

44 *Id.*

45 *Id.*

46 *Id.*

47 *Id.*

48 *Id.*

49 *Id.*

50 *Id.*

51 118 F.Supp.3d 1195 (D. Idaho. Aug. 3, 2015).

52 Idaho Code 18-7042.

53 Idaho Code 18-7042(3) & (4).

54 *Animal Legal Defense Fund*, 118 F.Supp.3d at 1200-01.

55 *Id.*

56 *Id.*

57 *Id.* at 1211-12.

58 *Id.* at 1201-02 (citing William A. Bloodworth, Jr., UPTON SINCLAIR 45-48 (1977). *See also* UPTON SINCLAIR, THE JUNGLE (1906).

59 *Animal Legal Defense Fund*, 118 F.Supp.3d at 1201-02.

60 *Id.* at 1202.

61 *Id.* at 1202.

62 *Id.* at 1208.

63 *Id.* at 1207.

64 *Id.* at 1202.

65 *Id.* at 1203.

66 *Id.* at 1204.

67 *Id.*

68 *Id.*

69 *Id.* at 1205.

70 *Id.*

71 *Id.* at 1205-06.

72 *Id.* at 1206.

73 Betsy Z. Russell, *Idaho appeals 'ag-gag' ruling to 9th Circuit*, available at: http://www.spokesman.com/blogs/boise/2015/dec/11/idaho-appeals-ag-gag-ruling-9th-circuit/.

74 Western Watersheds Project v. Michael, 196 F. supp.3d 1231 1248 (D. Wyo. July 6, 2016.

75 Wyo. Stat. § 6-3-414 (2016); Wyo. Stat. § 40-27-101 (2016).

76 *See Western Watersheds Project*, 196 F. supp. 3d at 1235-38.

77 *See id.* at 1241-42.

78 *See id.* at 1246.

79 *See id.*

80 *See* Brief of Amici Curiae Professors Brooke Kroeger et al., *supra* note 25, at 6-12.

81 *Id.* at 6-7 (citing BROOKE KROEGER, UNDERCOVER REPORTING: THE TRUTH ABOUT DECEPTION 3 (2012)).

Chapter 10

Invasion of Privacy

By Shaakirrah R. Sanders
Associate Professor of Law, University of Idaho

Overview

The right to privacy is defined as "the right to be let alone."[1] It would be incorrect to assume that this right dates back to English common law origins, like many other fundamental rights. In fact, "prior to 1890, no English or American court had ever expressly recognized the existence of the right" to privacy.[2]

In 1961, the Idaho Supreme Court for the first time recognized four categories of claims for invasion of privacy in *Peterson v. Idaho First National Bank.*[3] The first category are intrusions on seclusion or solitude, or into private affairs.[4] The second category is public disclosure of embarrassing, private facts.[5] The third category is publicity that presents a false light in public eyes.[6] The final category is an appropriation of one's name and likeness for the advantage of another.[7]

The four categories of claims for invasion of privacy recognized by Idaho parallel that described in the *Restatement (Second) of Torts.*[8] Section 652A of the *Restatement* describes how invasion of privacy has "clearly become crystallized and generally been held to be actionable as a matter of tort liability."[9] Section 652B discusses the first category–intrusion on seclusion or solitude, or into private affairs.[10] Section 652D discusses the second category–public disclosure of embarrassing, private facts.[11] Section 652E discusses the third category–false light.[12] Section 652C discusses the final category–appropriation of name and likeness.[13]

Idaho law and the *Restatement* also parallel on the type of damages that are recoverable for a claim for invasion of privacy. Section 652H establishes that a "cause of action for invasion of privacy, in any of its four forms, entitles the plaintiff to recover damages for the harm to the particular element of privacy that is invaded."[14] Additionally, an individual may also recover damages for emotional distress and personal humiliation, as long as it is of a kind that "normally results from such an invasion."[15] An individual may also recover any special damages that can be proved.[16]

The right to privacy—and any corollary claim for invasion of privacy—is personal and peculiar to the individual whose privacy is invaded.[17] As discussed in section 652I of the *Restatement*, the plaintiff whose privacy was invaded must be a living individual, unless the claim involved the final category – invasion by appropriation of name and likeness.[18] The cause of action for invasion of privacy is unassignable.[19] A person whose privacy has not been invaded cannot maintain a claim on behalf of a family member or any other person.[20] Additionally, in absence of a statute, the action for invasion of privacy also cannot be maintained after death (except with regards to the final category).[21] Nor does a corporation, partnership, or unincorporated association have a personal right to privacy, except to the extent that such entity has "a limited right to the exclusive use of its own name or identity in so far as they are of use or benefit, and it receives protection from the law of unfair competition."[22]

Idaho law recognizes that invasion of privacy claims against the media are limited by the First Amendment,[23] which applies a heightened standard referred to as the *New York Times* privilege. This standard was first announced in 1964 in *New York Times v. Sullivan*,[24] where the United States Supreme Court held that Alabama's libel law—and ultimately the libel laws of most states—was constitutionally deficient for failure to provide sufficient safeguards for freedom of speech and of the press.[25] The Court held that a libel action brought by a public official against critics of his official conduct required proof of actual malice.[26] The Court would ultimately extend the *New York Times* privilege to apply against public figures in *Curtis Publishing Co. v. Butts.*[27] The Court would later hold in *Gertz v. Robert Welch, Inc.*[28] that *New York Times* privilege also applied to punitive damages in a defamation case that involved the publication of information within the public's interest or concern. However, in *Dun & Bradstreet, Inc. v. Greenmoss Builders, Inc.*,[29] the Court held that the *New York Times* privilege did not apply to punitive damages in a defamation case that involved the publication of private information about a private figure. The *New York Times* privilege was extended to claims involving intentional infliction of emotional distress in *Hustler Magazine v. Fallwell.*[30] In *Times v. Hill*,[31] the Court applied the New York Times privilege to claims for invasion of privacy.

New York Times v. Sullivan involved a libel claim brought by L.B. Sullivan, who was one of three elected commissioners for Montgomery, Alabama.[32] The New York Times published an editorial on March 29, 1960 that claimed that African-Americans had suffered abuse for seeking the right-to-vote in Jim Crow Alabama.[33] None of the statements in the editorial mentioned the name of the commissioners.[34] However, Sullivan "contended that the word 'police' in the third paragraph referred to him as the Montgomery Commissioner who supervised the Police Department."[35] Sullivan concluded that the editorial could "be read as accusing the Montgomery police, and hence" Sullivan, of answering civil rights "protests with 'intimidation and violence,' bombing . . . homes, assaulting . . . persons, and charging [Dr. Martin Luther King] with perjury."[36] Testimony in the record from Sullivan "and six other Montgomery residents" supported the view that "some or all of the statements" referred to Sullivan "in his capacity as Commissioner."[37] After a trial, a jury awarded Sullivan $500,000 in damages.[38] The Alabama Supreme Court upheld the award.[39]

New York Times held that Alabama's libel law was constitutionally deficient.[40] The Court declared the cause of action for libel "must be measured by standards that satisfy the First Amendment," which protects the "unfettered interchange of ideas for the bringing about of political and social changes desired by the people.'"[41] The U.S. constitutional system encourages "free political discussion" to force government to respond "to the will of the people" in a way that is lawful and "essential to the security of the Republic."[42] The Court described the ability to speak one's mind as a "prized American privilege."[43] This privilege "presupposes that right conclusions are more likely to be gathered out of a multitude of tongues, than through any kind of authoritative selection."[44]

Turning its attention to Alabama's cause of action for libel, the *New York Times* Court fashioned a new "federal rule" or "privilege" for libel cases against the media.[45] That rule prohibited a "public official from recovering damages for a defamatory falsehood relating to his official conduct unless he proves that the statement was made with 'actual malice'—that is, with knowledge that it was false or with reckless disregard of whether it was false or not."[46] The rule—which has come to be known as the *New York Times* privilege—extends "to a great variety of subjects and includes matters of public concern, public men, and candidates for office."[47] This broad interpretation reflects the First Amendment's "profound national commitment to the principle that debate on public issues should be uninhibited, robust, and wide-open" and required tolerance of "vehement, caustic, and sometimes unpleasantly sharp attacks on government and public officials."[48] The Court noted that Alabama's libel statute allowed a presumption of malice on the issue of general damages.[49] This presumption was inconsistent with the new federal rule.[50] The Court therefore applied the *New York Times* privilege in all libel actions for damages against public officials.[51]

The question of whether the *New York Times* privilege also applied to public figures, not only public officials, was answered in the affirmative in 1967 in *Curtis Publishing Co. v. Butts* and its companion case, *Associated Press v. Walker*.[52] Seven years later, the court declined to apply the *New York Times* privilege to cases that did not involve a public official or figure. That case, *Gertz v. Robert Welch, Inc.*,[53] did hold that the *New York Times* privilege applied where presumed damages or punitive damages were sought and the matter was of public concern.[54] *Dunn & Bradstreet, Inc. v. Greenmoss Builders, Inc.*[55] re-examined *Gertz v. Robert Welch, Inc.* with regards to the application of the *New York Times* privilege to *presumed* and *punitive damages* in cases brought by a private individual where the alleged defamation did not involve an issue of public concern.[56] The Court declined to apply *New York Times v. Sullivan* privilege where there was neither a public official or figure nor an issue of public concern.[57]

Idaho also recognizes another First Amendment limitation that could apply to defamation claims against the media: the right to freely disclose and publish information discovered in public records. The United States Supreme Court announced this rule in 1975 in *Cox Broadcasting Corporation v. Cohn*.[58] This case involved the rape and murder of a 17-year-old girl, Cynthia Cohn.[59] Six minors, all of whom were male, were indicted.[60] Each pled guilty to rape and prosecutors dismissed the murder charges.[61] During a court hearing in the case, a television news reporter obtained a copy of the indictments from the court clerk.[62] In a subsequent broadcast the reporter revealed the victim's name, which the reporter obtained from the indictments.[63] A Georgia law prohibited publicizing or broadcasting a rape victim's name or identity.[64] Thus while the indictments were considered public records, until the broadcast Cohn's name had not been disclosed to the public.[65] After the broadcast Cohn's father brought a tort action for invasion of privacy against Cox Broadcasting, which owned the station that broadcast Cynthia Cohn's name.[66]

As in *New York Times*, the United States Supreme Court in *Cox Broadcasting Corporation* recognized that a tension exists between the First Amendment and certain privacy claims arising in tort.[67] The Court stressed that the media has a great responsibility to accurately and fully report news related to government operations.[68] Without accurate and full reports of government matters, most individuals would be unable make intelligent decisions on issues of public concern.[69] With respect to judicial proceedings, which are public events, the press serves to guarantee the fairness of trials.[70] The press also reveals to the public how courts administer justice.[71] Reflecting on the importance of fair trials and on the effective administration of justice, the Court held that trials were public events and that reports of those trials received special First Amendment protection.[72] In effect, making records public served an important interest because those records are of interest to individuals who are concerned with government administration.[73]

Cox Broadcasting Corporation declared a right or privilege to accurately and truthfully report information contained in public records.[74] Moreover, this privilege is not limited to information contained in judicial proceedings, but also other institutions of democratic government.[75] Thus, there is no right to suppress, edit, or censor courtroom events. Moreover, no privacy right is invaded by publication of information contained in reports of judicial proceedings.[76] Accordingly, liability for the press does not lie in publication of facts contained in unsealed public records.[77] The United States Supreme Court has upheld *Cox Broadcasting Corporation* on multiple occasions.[78]

This chapter outlines the four categories of invasion of privacy that are recognized by Idaho courts: (1) intrusion on seclusion or solitude, or into private affairs; (2) public disclosure of embarrassing, private facts; (3) publicity that presents a false light in public eyes; and (4) appropriation of one's name and likeness for the advantage of another. This chapter demonstrates how Idaho law parallels the *Restatement (Second) of Torts* and the First Amendment. This chapter also discusses *Taylor v. KTVB*[79] and *Uranga*,[80] which are the primary Idaho Supreme Court cases involving invasion of privacy claims against the media. Both cases involve the second category—public disclosure of embarrassing, private facts. *Uranga v. Federated Publications, Inc.* also touches upon the first and third categories— invasion of privacy by intrusion and by false light.

Category One: Intrusion on Seclusion or Solitude, or into Private Affairs

The first category of invasion of privacy the Idaho Supreme Court has recognized is a claim for intrusion on seclusion, solitude or into private affairs.[81] *The Restatement (Second) of Torts* § 652B describes invasion of privacy by intrusion as follows:

> "One who intentionally intrudes, physically or otherwise, upon the solitude or seclusion of another or his private affairs or concerns, is subject to liability to the other for invasion of privacy, if the intrusion would be highly offensive to a reasonable person."[82]

The *Restatement* explains that this claim involves intrusions into places in which the plaintiff has secluded themselves, such as a home or a hotel room.[83] However, the *Restatement* does not limit liability to intrusions into physical areas.[84] The intrusion may be by the use of one's senses, which may or may not involve mechanical aids to oversee or overhear private affairs.[85] An intrusion may be by looking into windows with binoculars or tapping telephone wires.[86] The intrusion may also be by some other form of investigation or examination.[87] Examples given in the *Restatement* include opening private and personal mail, searching a safe or wallet, or examining private bank accounts.[88] Under the right circumstances, these could subject a defendant to liability even though there is no publication or other use of the information.[89]

The Idaho Supreme Court has discussed other types of activities that are sufficient (or insufficient) to bring a cause of action against the media for invasion of privacy by intrusion in *Uranga v. Federated Publications, Inc.*[90] This case involved a front-page story that was printed in the Idaho Statesman.[91] That story featured the 1955-56 "Boys of Boise Scandal," which involved the alleged propositioning of teenage boys by adult homosexual men at a Boise YMCA.[92] In connection with the investigation, law enforcement interrogated approximately 1,500 individuals[93] and arrested 16 individuals.[94] The Statesman story centered on Frank Jones,[95] who was the son of a city council member and a student at the United States Military Academy at West Point.[96] While at West Point, Jones accused Melvin Dir of sexual assault. Dir denied Jones' allegation.[97] In an unsworn written statement, Dir also described how after their sexual encounter Jones admitted to other gay affairs.[98] One of those admitted affairs was with Uranga, Jones' cousin.[99] The Statesman did not provide Uranga's name in the body of the story.[100] However, the Statesman did reprint the entirety of Dir's unsworn written statement, which mentioned Uranga's name.[101] Fred Uranga requested that the Statesman retract his name from the unsworn statement.[102] When the Statesman refused, Fred Uranga brought a lawsuit for infliction of emotional distress, as well as three claims for invasion of privacy, which included invasion of privacy by intrusion, by disclosure of private facts, and by false light.[103]

Uranga declared that the claim for invasion of privacy by intrusion requires an intentional interference with the plaintiff's interest in solitude or seclusion, either as to his person or as to his private affairs or concerns.[104]

"This form of invasion of privacy does not depend upon the publicity given to the person whose interest" was invaded or exposed.[105] All that is necessary is that the prying or intrusion be of a type that would be offensive to a reasonable person.[106] *Uranga* also illustrates how a successful claim for this category of invasion of privacy requires a substantial intrusion.[107] As section 652B of the *Restatement* explains, such an intrusion must be "of a kind that would be highly offensive to the ordinary reasonable man, as the result of conduct to which the reasonable man would strongly object."[108] The *Restatement* gives the following example:

> [T]here is no liability for knocking at the plaintiff's door, or calling him to the telephone on one occasion or even two or three, to demand payment of a debt. It is only when the telephone calls are repeated with such persistence and frequency as to amount to a course of hounding the plaintiff, that [such demands] becomes a substantial burden to his existence, that his privacy is invaded.[109]

Uranga maintained that an "examination of a public record cannot be the basis of a claim for invasion of privacy by intrusion."[110] The court ultimately found that Uranga did not and could not allege an intrusion into a place of solitude or seclusion because the publication was based on information that was contained in and obtained from records that were open to the public.[111] This case demonstrates that in Idaho, the media (and the public) have open access to report on matters contained in unsealed public records.

Category Two: Public Disclosure of Embarrassing, Private Facts

The second category of invasion of privacy that the Idaho Supreme Court recognizes is where there has been public disclosure of embarrassing or private facts. *The Restatement (Second) of Torts* § 652D describes invasion of privacy by public disclosure as follows:

> "One who gives publicity to a matter concerning the private life of another is subject to liability to the other for invasion of his privacy, if the matter publicized is of a kind that (a) would be highly offensive to a reasonable person, and (b) is not of legitimate concern to the public."[112]

The *Restatement* labels this claim as "Publicity Given to Private Life."[113] The comments to this section of the *Restatement* warn about an inconsistency with the First Amendment to the extent that this section allows for tort liability for publicity given to true statements of fact.[114]

Idaho courts have outlined three elements for invasion of privacy by public disclosure. The first element is that there be publicity.[115] The second element is that the publicity must be of private, not public facts.[116] The final element is that the matter made public must be one that "would be offensive and objectionable to a reasonable man of ordinary sensibilities."[117]

To interpret the first element – publicity – Idaho courts rely on the *Restatement*, which makes clear that invasion of privacy by public disclosure requires more than publication to third parties.[118] In this sense, the *Restatement* defines publication as "any communication by the defendant to a third party."[119] Instead, invasion of privacy by public disclosure requires publicity.[120] Publicity involves making the matter "public, by communicating it to the public at large, or to so many persons that the matter must be regarded as substantially certain to become one of public knowledge."[121] According to the Restatement, the difference between publicity and publication is not "the means of communication."[122] Rather, the distinction is between private and public communication.[123] Thus any communication, whether it be oral, written, or by any other means, that reaches or is sure to reach, the public could be considered publicity.[124] The publicity/publication distinction also exists for the third category of claims for invasion of privacy (that by false light).[125]

To interpret the second element – disclosure of private facts[126] – Idaho courts again turn to the *Restatement*, which imposes liability only where the publicity concerns matters that are private, as distinguished from the public life of an individual.[127] In other words, there is no liability where the defendant "gives further publicity to information about the plaintiff that is already public."[128] Nor is there liability where the plaintiff leaves themselves "open to the public eye" or where the plaintiff's activities occur in a public place.[129] Moreover, where matters are of a legitimate public interest, there may be no actionable invasion of privacy by public disclosure even if the matter concerns the intimate details of one's life.[130]

To interpret the third element – offensiveness to a reasonable person of ordinary sensibilities[131] – Idaho courts, like the *Restatement*, require the publication to be unreasonable.[132] Thus, the public disclosure "must be relative to the customs of the time and place, to the occupation of the plaintiff and to the habits of his neighbors and fellow citizens."[133] As explained by the *Restatement*, minor and moderate annoyances are insufficient to give rise to invasion of privacy by public disclosure.[134] The publicity must be such that a reasonable person would feel seriously aggrieved.[135] Even in this case, if the publicity is of a matter of legitimate public concern, there is no invasion of privacy by public disclosure.[136] Moreover, for both voluntary and involuntary public figures, the legitimate interests of the public may extend to matters that would otherwise be private.[137] A legitimate interest may also extend beyond the events that aroused the public's interest.[138]

Even where a plaintiff can make a sufficient showing on the three elements for invasion of privacy by public disclosure, Idaho courts and the *Restatement* give the media a great deal of leeway to determine what to disseminate to the public.[139] That leeway may extend to family members or other persons closely associated with the voluntary or involuntary public figure.[140] However, the *Restatement* draws a line where the publicity ceases to concern information to which the public is entitled.[141] As a result, the media may be liable where publicity becomes a morbid and sensational prying into one's private life simply for its own sake (or into matters of which there is no public concern).[142] Additionally, the scope of a matter of legitimate concern to the public extends to "the use of names, likenesses or facts in giving information to the public for purposes of education, amusement or enlightenment."[143] A "lapse of time" between the publicity and the event that made the plaintiff a public figure "does not defeat the authority to give . . . or renew publicity."[144] This rule applies even where the lapse of time is considerable.[145]

Taylor v. KTVB[146] is one of the leading Idaho cases involving invasion of privacy by public disclosure against the media. In 1974, KTVB aired the arrest of Oren Taylor, who had allegedly threatened his sister and his female housekeeper with a gun.[147] The women made a complaint to 911, who immediately dispatched law enforcement officers to Taylor's home.[148] KTVB reporters, who had been monitoring the police frequencies, heard the 911 call to the police and sent a cameraperson to the scene.[149] Law enforcement ultimately ordered Taylor from his home and arrested him.[150] Unfortunately, Taylor had been sleeping in the nude and did not have an opportunity to clothe himself before leaving his home.[151] The KTVB cameraperson captured Taylor's nudity, which appeared for less than a second during the next day's evening news.[152]

Taylor subsequently brought an action alleging that KTVB invaded his privacy by publicly disclosing embarrassing or private facts.[153] A jury awarded Taylor $15,000, but the Idaho Supreme Court reversed the award.[154] The failure to instruct the jury about the appropriate standard for news media who are accused of invasion of privacy constituted primary ground for the reversal.[155] KTVB argued, among other things, that the trial court should have instructed the jury that liability arose in only three situations.[156] First, if the event published was not "newsworthy."[157] Second, if the publisher had "actual knowledge that the incident would be highly offensive."[158] Third, if the publisher acted with "reckless disregard of whether it would be offensive."[159] The court agreed with KTVB and held that in accordance with *New York Times v. Sullivan*, [160] the trial court should have instructed the jury on the malice requirement.[161]

Taylor immediately recognized the parallels between Idaho's cause of action for invasion of privacy by public disclosure and the heightened First Amendment standard set forth by the United States Supreme Court in *New York Times*. The Idaho Supreme Court recognized the unquestionable right to receive and disseminate news about matters that are in the public's interest.[162] This includes crimes and those accused of committing crimes.[163] In short, "reports of governmental action in criminal matters are the legitimate province of a free press."[164] Those accused of crimes "are the objects of legitimate public interest," at least during that period of time their conduct brought them to the public's attention.[165] The court also relied upon the *Restatement*, which provides that "persons charged with crimes 'are the objects of legitimate public interest during the period of time after their conduct . . . has brought them to public attention."[166] The court also looked to California law, which maintained that "there can be no doubt that reports of current criminal activities are the legitimate province of a free press."[167]

The First Amendment's heightened protection also applies to "newsworthy" events and *Taylor* announced a broad definition of what events were "newsworthy."[168] 'News' includes all events and items of information that are out of the ordinary humdrum routine."[169] News also includes information that has the definable quality of arousing "public attention."[170] Here the court declares that the press has the ability to make its own definition of news, which extends to all matters of genuine and popular appeal, even if the appeal is more or less "deplorable."[171]

Taylor acknowledged that because of the First Amendment, some individuals will lose or have lost privacy rights simply because they were "caught up and entangled" in the "web of news and public interest."[172] The court also warned that cases are "not to be tried in the papers."[173] However, the overriding social interest in encouraging unknown individuals to come forward with useful information to identify and locate suspects and victims of crimes supports public dissemination of information about a case.[174] Public dissemination could also encourage eye- and character witnesses to testify in court.[175] Thus, those who are caught up in newsworthy events become "public figures for a season," or at least until the individual pivots back to his or her lawful and unexciting life.[176] For that season, those individuals are subject to public scrutiny by publishers who wish to "satisfy the curiosity of the public as to their leaders, heroes, villains, and victims."[177] In this context, the societal interest in news outweighs the individual right to privacy.[178]

Almost 30 years after *Taylor*, the Idaho Supreme Court affirmed the alignment between the First Amendment and invasion of privacy claims against the media. As discussed, *Uranga v. Federated Publications, Inc.*[179] concerned a front-page story printed in the Idaho Statesman that featured the 1955-56 "Boys of Boise Scandal."[180] Frank Jones, who was featured in the story, allegedly confessed to a sexual encounter with his cousin, Fred Uranga.[181] Although that alleged confession was contained in public records, Uranga brought a cause of action for invasion of privacy by public disclosure, as well as causes of action for invasion of privacy by intrusion and by false light.[182] On this issue, *Uranga* followed the rule set forth by *Cox Broadcasting Corporation v. Cohn*, which prohibited invasion of privacy claims that are based on truthful reporting of facts contained in public records.[183] The Idaho Supreme Court ultimately held that Fred Uranga's cause of action was indistinguishable from those presented in *Cox Broadcasting Corporation.*[184]

Uranga also demonstrates how there is no expiration date on what is considered "news" that is in the public's interest. The 1995 Idaho Stateman's article at issue in *Uranga* concerned a scandal that originally occurred in 1955.[185] As explained in the *Restatement:*

> The fact that there has been a lapse of time, even of consid-

> erable length, since the event that has made the plaintiff a public figure, does not itself defeat the authority to give him publicity or to renew publicity when it has formerly been given. Past events and activities may still be of legitimate interest to the public, and a narrative reviving recollection of what has happened even many years ago may be both interesting and valuable for purposes of information and education.[186]

The *Restatement* clarifies that the question depends on community standards or norms.[187] One factor for consideration should include "whether the publicity goes to unreasonable lengths in revealing facts about one who has resumed the private, lawful and unexciting life led by the great bulk of the community."[188]

Category Three: Publicity that Presents a False Light in Public Eyes

The third category of invasion of privacy that is recognized by Idaho courts is where publicity places a person in a false light in the public eyes. The *Restatement (Second) of Torts* § 652E describes invasion of privacy by false light as follows:

> One who gives publicity to a matter concerning another that places the other before the public in a false light is subject to liability to the other for invasion of his privacy if: (a) the false light in which the other was placed would be highly offensive to a reasonable person, and (b) the actor had knowledge of or acted in reckless disregard as to the falsity of the publicized matter and the false light in which the other would be placed.[189]

The *Restatement* clarifies that claims for invasion of privacy by false light must involve untruths.[190] Moreover, there must be publicity of those untrue matters.[191]

Invasion of privacy by false light shares some commonalities with the second category of invasion of privacy (that by public disclosure).[192] The *Restatement* again distinguishes between publicity and publication, the former being the first element of invasion of privacy by public disclosure.[193] The distinction lies between that which is considered a private communication and that which is considered a public communication.[194] Any communication that reaches, or is sure to reach, the public could be considered publicity, whether it be oral, written or by any other means.[195] Publication is defined as "any communication by the defendant to a third party."[196] Publicity occurs when matters are "made public, by communicating it to the public at large, or to so many persons that the matter must be regarded as substantially certain to become one of public knowledge."[197] The type of publicity required for invasion of privacy by false light must be of a kind that would be highly offensive to a reasonable person.[198] The *Restatement* provides that minor errors or unimportant details would not in absence of special circumstances give rise to invasion of privacy by false light.[199] Only "major misrepresentations" of character, history, activities, or beliefs give rise to a cause of action.[200] *Uranga v. Federated Publications, Inc.*[201] is somewhat illustrative of invasion of privacy by false light. As discussed above, Frank Uranga brought a lawsuit after the Idaho Statesman refused to move his name from a story that cast light on his sexuality.[202] Uranga ultimately abandoned this claim and acknowledged that the media was not required to independently verify all allegations found in a court record before publication.[203]

When publicity given to the plaintiff is also defamatory, the plaintiff may bring causes of action for both defamation (see Chapter 4) and invasion of privacy by false light.[204] Defamation and invasion of privacy by false light are separate and distinct torts, comprised of separate and distinct elements.[205] Thus, if one proceeds to bring both claims, invasion of privacy by false light would not require a showing of defamation.[206] The *Restatement* explains it is sufficient that an individual be given such unreasonable and highly objectionable publicity that certain false attributes are associated with that individual's characteristics, conduct or beliefs and that the individual is placed before the public in a false position.[207] The *Restatement* describes the distinction between a cause of action for invasion of privacy by false light and defamation as follows: with defamation, the primary interest to be protected is one's public reputation or status, whereas with invasion of privacy by false light the interest to be protected is essentially the plaintiff's own peace of mind.[208] Where one successfully proves both defamation and invasion of privacy by false light, only one recovery is allowed for "each single instance of publicity."[209]

Steele v. Spokesman-Review[210] provides an example of the intersection between invasion of privacy by false light and defamation.[211] This case involved a publication in The Spokesman-Review about Edgar Steele, who filed a notice of substitution of counsel to represent several members of the Aryan Nations in a civil cause of action for assault.[212] The Spokesman-Review reported that Steele was previously acquainted with two founders of a white supremacist group and that he moved from California to Idaho around the same time as several other members of that group.[213] After The Spokesman-Review rebuffed his request to retract the article, Steele brought a lawsuit for defamation, invasion of privacy, and intentional infliction of emotional distress.[214] The lawsuit alleged that The Spokesman-Review article contained statements that were untrue or statements that falsely depicted Steele as a white supremacist by insinuation and innuendo.[215]

The Idaho Supreme Court's analysis in *Steele* focuses more on defamation than invasion of privacy by false light. On the issue of defamation, the court held that media defendants are not required to show the "literal truth" in order to successfully defend a claim for defamation or invasion of privacy by false light.[216] As long as the "charge is true in substance," a court will view "[s]light inaccuracies of expression" as immaterial.[217] In Idaho, minor inaccuracies do not amount to falsity as "long as the substance, the gist, the sting of the allegedly libelous charge be justified."[218] Edgar Steele was unable to show the contested statements were untrue because much of the evidence contradicted his claim.[219] Steele did take over the representation of the Aryan Nations.[220] Steele also participated in the public debate over the case.[221] Finally, Steele was unable to show that any errors contained in the publication were more than "slight inaccuracies."[222] On the issue of invasion of privacy, the court held that an essential element was whether there was a "public disclosure of falsity or fiction concerning the plaintiff."[223] Steele was denied recovery because the facts disclosed in the The Spokesman-Review's article were readily available from public sources.[224]

Category Four: Appropriation of Name and Likeness for the Advantage of Another

The final category of invasion of privacy that the Idaho Supreme Court recognizes is where one's name and likeness has been appropriated for the advantage of another.[225] *The Restatement (Second) of Torts* § 652C describes invasion of privacy by appropriation as follows:

> "One who appropriates to his own use or benefit the name or likeness of another is subject to liability to the other for invasion of privacy."[226]

Invasion of privacy by appropriation protects the exclusive use of one's own identity to the extent that identity is represented by one's own name or likeness.[227] By its nature, this category of invasion of privacy is a type of property right.[228]

The *Restatement* recognizes that "an exclusive license may be given to a third person, which will entitle the licensee to maintain an action to protect it."[229] The types of activities that constitute invasion of privacy by appropriation include the appropriation of an individual's name or likeness for commercial purposes, such as an advertisement.[230] However, not all states limit causes of action to appropriations for commercial purposes.[231] Nor do all states require the appropriation to have a pecuniary purpose.[232]

This cause of action requires an appropriation of "the reputation, prestige, social or commercial standing, public interest or other values of" another's name or likeness.[233] The *Restatement* explains that it is not enough that one adopts for themselves a name that is the same as that of another.[234] There must also be evidence that one has passed themselves off as another person or otherwise sought to obtain for themselves the value or benefits of the other person's name or identity.[235] In this sense, neither the *Restatement* nor Idaho law will impose liability unless or until "the value of the name has in some way been appropriated."[236] The *Restatement* also makes clear that if there is no "such appropriation, the defendant is free to call himself by any name . . . whether there is only one person or a thousand others of the same name."[237] The Restatement also requires invasion of privacy by appropriation to involve more than a mere mention of or reference to another's name or likeness.[238] Nor does liability lie merely because one's name or likeness was brought before the public.[239] Liability requires publicity that is "given for the purpose of appropriating to the defendant's benefit the commercial or other values associated with the name or the likeness."[240] The fact that one is engaged in the publication of a newspaper for profit is alone insufficient to impose liability for the incidental publication of a commercial use of another's name or likeness.[241] In other words, a newspaper or other media organization is not liable for invasion by appropriation merely because they have published another person's name or likeness.[242]

As explained in the *Overview* to this Chapter, invasion of privacy by appropriation does not require a living plaintiff. [243] Thus, unlike the other three categories of invasion of privacy, an individual whose privacy has been invaded by appropriation can assign their claim.[244] A corporation, partnership, or unincorporated association may also bring a cause of action for invasion by appropriation, in addition to other types of causes of action that protect the company from unfair competition or unauthorized uses of the company's name or identity.[245]

Conclusion

Idaho, like most states, recognizes four categories of claims for invasion of privacy. The first category are intrusions on seclusion or solitude, or into private affairs. The second category is public disclosure of embarrassing, private facts. The third category is publicity that presents a false light in public eyes. The final category is an appropriation of one's name and likeness for the advantage of another. *Taylor v. KTVB* and *Uranga v. Federated Publications, Inc.* are the primary Idaho Supreme Court cases involving invasion of privacy claims against the media. Both cases demonstrate the parallels between the Idaho law and the Restatement. Both cases also demonstrate the influence of *New York Times v. Sullivan*, which interpreted the First Amendment to require a public official or figure to prove "actual malice" to recover general, presumed, and punitive damages. The privilege also requires a private individual to prove actual malice to recover presumed and punitive damages if the media's publication involved an issue of public concern. Idaho also recognizes the First Amendment privilege announced in *Cox Broadcasting Corporation v. Cohn* that allows free disclosure or publication of information contained in public records.

Endnotes

1 *Restatement (Second) of Torts* § 652A cmt. a (Am. Law Inst. 1975).

2 *Id.*

3 83 Idaho 578 (1961).

4 Taylor v. K.T.V.B., Inc., 96 Idaho 202, 203 (1974).

5 *Id.*

6 *Id.*

7 *Id.*

8 *Restatement (Second) of Torts* (Am. Law Inst. 1975).

9 *Id.* at § 652A cmt. c.

10 *Id.* at § 652B.

11 *Id.* at § 652D.

12 *Id.* at § 652E.

13 *Id.* at § 652C.

14 *Id.* at § 652H cmt. a.

15 *Id.* at § 652H cmt. b.

16 *Id.* at § 652H(c).

17 *Id.* at § 652I cmt. a.

18 *Id.* at § 652I.

19 *Id.* at § 652I cmt. a.

20 *Id.*

21 *Id.* at § 652I cmt. b.

22 *Id.* at § 652I cmt. c, See generally *Federal Communications Commission v. AT&T*, 526 U.S. 397 (2011).

23 U.S. Const. amend. I.

24 376 U.S. 254 (1964).

25 *New York Times*, 376 U.S. at 256, 264-65, 267-68.

26 *Id.* at 279-82.

27 338 U.S. 130 (1967).

28 418 U.S. 323 (1974).

29 472 U.S. 749 (1985).

30 Hustler Magazine v. Falwell, 483 U.S. 46 (1988).

31 385 U.S. 374 (1967).

32 *New York Times*, 376 U.S. 254, 256 (1964).

33 *Id.* at 256-61.

34 *Id.* at 258.

35 *Id.*

36 *Id.*

37 *Id.*

38 *Id*. at 256.

39 *Id*.

40 *Id*. at 264-65.

41 *Id*. at 269.

42 *Id*.

43 *Id*.

44 *Id*.

45 *Id*. at 279.

46 *Id*. at 279-80.

47 *Id*. at 281-82.

48 *Id*. at 270.

49 *Id*. at 283.

50 *Id*. at 283-84.

51 *Id*. at 284.

52 388.U.S. 130 (1967).

53 418 U.S. 323 (1974).

54 *Id.* at 349-50.

55 472 U.S. 749 (1985).

56 *Id.* at 759-61.

57 *Id*. at 757-62.

58 420 U.S. 469 (1975).

59 *Cox Broadcasting Corp*., 420 U.S. at 471, 472 n.2.

60 *Id.* at 471.

61 *Id.* at 472.

62 *Id.*

63 *Id.* at 473.

64 *Id.* at 471-74.

65 *Id.*

66 *Id.* at 474.

67 *Id.* at 487-91.

68 *Id.* at 491-92.

69 *Id.*

70 *Id.* at 492.

71 *Id.*

72 *Id.*

73 *Id.*

74 *Id.* at 493-95.

75 *Id.* at 492-93.

76 *Id.*

77 *Id.* at 493-95.

78 *See generally Oklahoma Publishing v. Oklahoma County District Court*, 430 U.S. 308 (1977); *Landmark Communications, Inc. v. Virginia*, 435 U.S. 829 (1978); *Smith v. Daily Mail Publishing Company*, 443 U.S. 97 (1979); *Florida Star v. B.J.F.*, 491 U.S. 524 (1989).

79 96 Idaho 202 (1974).

80 138 Idaho 550 (2003).

81 Taylor v. K.T.V.B., Inc., 96 Idaho 202, 203 (1974).

82 *Restatement (Second) of Torts* § 652B (Am. Law Inst. 1975).

83 *Id.* at § 652B cmt. b.

84 *Id.*

85 *Id.*

86 *Id.*

87 *Id.*

88 *Id.*

89 *Id.*

90 138 Idaho 550 (2003).

91 *Uranga*, 138 Idaho at 551-52.

92 *Id.* at 551.

93 *Id.* at 551-52.

94 *Id.*

95 *Id.* at 552.

96 *Id.*

97 *Id.*

98 *Id.*

99 *Id.*

100 *Id.*

101 *Id.*

102 *Id.*

103 *Id.* at 553.

104 *Id.*

105 *Id.*

106 *Id.*

107 *Id.*

108 *Restatement (Second) of Torts* § 652B cmt. d (Am. Law Inst. 1975).

109 *Id.*

110 *Uranga*, 138 Idaho at 553 (citing Baker v. Burlington Northern, Inc., 99 Idaho 688 (1978) & *Restatement (Second) of Torts* § 652B cmt. c (Am. Law Inst. 1975)). *See also Uranga*, 138 Idaho at 554-56.

111 *Uranga*, 138 Idaho at 553.

112 *Restatement (Second) of Torts* § 652D (Am. Law Inst. 1975).

113 *Id.*

114 *Id.* at cmt. a.

115 Peterson v. Idaho First Nat'l Bank, 83 Idaho 578, 691 (1961).

116 *Id.*

117 *Id.*

118 *Restatement (Second) of Torts* § 652D cmt. a (Am. Law Inst. 1975).

119 *Id.*

120 *Id.*

121 *Id.*

122 *Id.*

123 *Id.*

124 *Id.*

125 *See generally id.* at § 652E and *id.* at § 652E cmts a.-f.

126 *Peterson*, 83 Idaho at 691.

127 *Restatement (Second) of Torts* § 652D cmt. b (Am. Law Inst. 1975).

128 *Id.*

129 *Id.*

130 *Id.*

131 *Peterson*, 83 Idaho at 691.

132 *Restatement (Second) of Torts* § 652D cmt. c (Am. Law Inst. 1975).

133 *Id.*

134 *Id.*

135 *Id.*

136 *Id.* at § 652D cmt. d.

137 *Id.* at § 652D cmt. e & f.

138 *Id.*

139 *Id.* at § 652D cmt. g.

140 *Id.* at § 652D cmt. i.

141 *Id.* at § 652D cmt. h.

142 *Id.*

143 *Id.* at § 652D cmt. j.

144 *Id.* at § 652D cmt. k.

145 *Id.*

146 96 Idaho 202 (1974).

147 *Taylor*, 96 Idaho at 202-03.

148 *Id.* at 203.

149 *Id.*

150 *Id.*

151 *Id.*

152 *Id.*

153 *Id.*

154 *Id.*

155 *Id.* at 203-04.

156 *Id.* at 204.

157 *Id.*

158 *Id.*

159 *Id.*

160 376 U.S. 254 (1964).

161 *Taylor*, 96 Idaho at 204.

162 *Id.*

163 *Id.*

164 *Id.*

165 *Id.* at 204-05.

166 *Id.* at 204.

167 *Id.* (citing Briscoe v. Readers Digest Ass'n, 4 Cal. 529 (1971)).

168 *Taylor*, 96 Idaho at 204.

169 *Id.*

170 *Id.*

171 *Id.*

172 *Id.*

173 *Id.* at 205.

174 *Id.*

175 *Id.*

176 *Id.* at 204.

177 *Id.* at 205 (citing *Restatement (Second) of Torts* § 652D cmt. f (Am. Law Inst. 1975).

178 *Taylor*, 96 Idaho at 205.

179 138 Idaho 550 (2003).

180 *Uranga*, 138 Idaho at 551-52.

181 *Id.* at 552.

182 *Id.*

183 *Id.* at 553-56.

184 *Id.* at 556.

185 *Id.* at 551.

186 *Restatement (Second) of Torts* § 652D cmt. k (Am. Law Inst. 1975).

187 *Id.*

188 *Id.*

189 *Id.* at § 652E.

190 *Id.* at § 652E cmt. a.

191 *Id.*

192 *See id.* (referring to *id.* at § 652D cmt. ac).

193 *See id.* at § 652D cmt. a.

194 *Id.*

195 *Id.*

196 *Id.*

197 *Id.*

198 *See id.* at § 652E cmt. c.

199 *Id.*

200 *Id.*

201 138 Idaho 550 (2003).

202 *Uranga*, 138 Idaho at 551-52.

203 *Id.* at 553.

204 *Restatement (Second) of Torts* § 652E cmt. b (Am. Law Inst. 1975).

205 *Id.*

206 *Id.*

207 *Id.*

208 *Id.*

209 *Id.*

210 138 Idaho 249 (2002).

211 *Steele,* 138 Idaho at 250.

212 *Id.* at 250-51.

213 *Id.* at 250.

214 *Id.*

215 *Id.*

216 *Id.* at 253.

217 *Id.*

218 *Id.*

219 *Id.*

220 *Id.*

221 *Id.*

222 *Id.*

223 *Id.*

224 *Id.* at 253.

225 Peterson v. Idaho First Nat'l Bank, 83 Idaho 578, 691 ((1961).

226 *Restatement (Second) of Torts* § 652C (Am. Law Inst. 1975).

227 *Id.* at § 652C cmt. a.

228 *Id.*

229 *Id.*

230 *Id.* at § 652C cmt. b.

231 *Id.*

232 *Id.*

233 *Id.* at § 652C cmt. c.

234 *Id.*

235 *Id.*

236 *Id.*

237 *Id.*

238 *Id.* at § 652C cmt. d.

239 *Id.*

240 *Id.*

241 *Id.*

242 *Id.*

243 *Id.* at § 652I cmt. b.

244 *Id.*

245 *Id.* at § 652I cmt. c.

Chapter 11

Native American Press Laws in Idaho

By Rebecca J. Tallent, Ed.D.
Associate Professor of Journalism, University of Idaho

Although Native American tribal lands are within the United States, the laws on those lands can vary greatly from the rest of U.S. law – and media law is no exception.

While most of the country's journalists rely on the First Amendment as the bedrock of the profession, Native American journalists may or may not have the same privilege. It all depends on the tribe's constitution and laws passed by the tribal government. Of the country's 566 federally recognized tribes fewer than half have freedom of the press, and those with press freedoms may or may not include anyone other than a Native American (Tallent & Dingman, 2011).

In Idaho, the three largest tribes – Coeur d'Alene, Nez Perce and Shoshone-Bannock – all have news outlets, but the laws governing each outlet are different. None of the Idaho tribes include outside media agencies in their media laws, which can be interpreted by the tribal government as not recognizing outside media; most of the tribal governments know they do not have to play by the same rules as local, state and federal governments when it comes to mainstream news reporting.

On occasion, this creates a serious problem for the tribe as mainstream journalists do not understand why they cannot cover a news story. In 2012, KIFI-TV news in Idaho Falls was preparing to do a story on tribal grounds about money from a federal lawsuit being distributed among tribal members. Although the TV station was told no distribution was happening that day, a reporter went to the reservation to cover the story and found distribution was happening, and the reporter was told to leave (News staff, 2012). As the TV station reported about their journalist Jake Taylor (News staff, 2012):

> Within a minute of setting up his camera, Jake was politely, but firmly, told to pack up and get out.
> "You have to stop. You have to cut your film. Why's that? Council put a hold on any type of filming for TV for this. It's just because we're getting too much negativity from the outside about what's going on. So we're trying to control it."

Because each tribe is a sovereign nation, each one has its own laws governing the nation and media laws vary from tribe to tribe. Tribes consider sovereignty a sacred right that is inherited from their ancestors and the Great Creator. Native press law is complex because it is also tied to many laws and court decisions involving Native Americans, but many of the laws do not seem to have any relationship to media unless they are viewed within the context of how the U.S. government has perceived all American Indian issues (Tallent & Dingman, 2011).

The first landmark case in Native American media law was the 1831 United States Supreme Court decision in *Cherokee Nation v. Georgia*, in which the court ruled the

Cherokee Nation is neither a state of the union or a foreign state, but a domestic independent nation (Marshall, 1831; Johnson, 1982). In 1832, the high court again ruled in favor of tribes when in the *Worcester v. Georgia* decision the court upheld the sovereignty of the Cherokee Nation and granted full governing power of tribal affairs to tribal government (Johnson, 1982). In addition, the Worcester ruling also recognized only the federal government has the power to deal with tribes and pass laws affecting tribal lands. To date, the principles of these two cases have been upheld (Worcester was overturned in 2001 by *Nevada Hicks*, but the premise of tribal sovereignty remains), recognizing tribal governments as being able to create laws to protect their citizens and create rule of law.

By 1968, Congress passed the Indian Civil Rights Act, which allowed tribes to include articles found in the U.S. Constitution to tribal constitutions; but the 1976 landmark U.S. Supreme Court case *Santa Clara Pueblo v. Martinez*, (98 S.Ct. 1670, 436 U.S. 49, 56, L.Ed.2nd. 106, 1978) made adding the freedoms optional. Under Martinez, tribal leaders could decide which freedoms to include and which ones to avoid (Brownstein, McDonald & Menikoff, 1977).

Although the first recorded Native newspaper, the Cherokee Phoenix, began printing in 1828 (Murphy, 1998), Native media did not find a boom period until 1960 through 1970 when President Lyndon Johnson's Great Society project helped to establish the Elementary and Secondary Education Act of 1965, which encouraged federal funding and more tribal publications (Littlefield & Parins, 1984). Native American news media outlets, both print and electronic (radio and television plus Internet) have been growing steadily since 1980, primarily due to three factors: economic growth in tribal communities; increased professionalism among Native American reporters and editors; and a heightened sense of tribal sovereignty (Loew & Mella, 2005).

Legally, some tribes (notably the Cherokee of Oklahoma and the Navajo Nation) have adopted Press Freedom Acts which provide First Amendment and other freedoms for tribal journalists (Tallent & Dingman, 2011), the Osage Nation was the first to enact a shield law for its reporters and the Cherokee of Oklahoma was the first nation to enact a Freedom of Information law (Tallent, 2012).

There are six federally recognized tribes in Idaho, and four of the six have a media presence, showing Native American news media is alive and expanding in the state with tribes establishing radio stations to complement their newspapers. One tribe – the Coeur d'Alene – is planning a television station in the future. To date, the Coeur d'Alene Tribe has a newspaper, the Council Fires; radio station KWIS as well as Red Spectrum Communications, an internet provider service; plus the tribe has actively used YouTube as a broadcast unit. About 100 miles to the south, the Nez Perce tribe has a newspaper, Ta'c Tito'oqan; radio station KIYE; and a wireless internet provider for its citizens. Further south in Fort Hall, the Shoshone-Bannock Tribes has the Sho-Ban News newspaper. In the far south, the Shoshone-Paiute Nation, which traverses the southwest Idaho-northern Nevada border, has the Sho-Pai News. As of July 2016, neither the Kootenai Tribe of Idaho near Bonners Ferry nor the Northwestern band of the Shoshone Nation (in Pocatello) have any news media outlets.

While at least two of the three tribes are expanding their media reach, none of the tribes have a specific Press Freedom Act nor do their laws include any media law outside of the tribe's constitution. The Nez Perce, Shoshone-Bannock, Shoshone-Paiute and Kootenai constitutions mirror the U.S. Constitution in media language with a First Amendment-style clause while the Coeur d'Alene constitution does not; however, the implementation of the clause is up to the existing respective councils to enforce. Specifics for each tribe follows. One note: although three of the tribes are Shoshone, these are three distinctly different tribes or bands with their own separate constitutions.

Coeur d'Alene Tribe or Schitsu'umsh

In the Coeur d'Alene Tribal Code (2012), there are clearly provisions for public gatherings and open air assemblies and religious freedom, but no specific press or media freedom. Still, the tribe has a newspaper which publishes tribal news each month and is under the tribe's Public Affairs Division, plus the radio station and internet provider for tribal members. There are likewise no provisions for press freedom in the tribe's constitution and bylaws (2012).

However, Council Fires editor Jennifer Fletcher said her newspaper is more like a small town paper than a public relations tool for the tribe. As she explained to Tallent & Dingman in 2011:

> Our council doesn't interfere. The previous editor had a lot of interference, but since I've taken over I've only been asked not to run something once; they wanted to wait until a court case was final, and it was more of a suggestion. Like any journalist, there are some things they won't tell me such as legal settlements, but it's really not an issue. My goal is to provide information through our paper.

Nez Perce Tribe or Nimiipuu

In its Tribal Code (2000), the Nez Perce have a specific clause which repeats much of the First Amendment:

> The Nez Perce Tribe in exercise of its sovereign powers of self-government shall not:
>
> > (a) Make or enforce any law prohibiting the free exercise of religion, or abridging the freedom of speech, or of the press, or the right of the people peaceably to assemble and to petition the tribal council for a redress of grievances.

Beyond this, tribal attorney Julie Kane (personal conversation of June 30, 2016) said while there is an internal memo concerning media policy, there are no other laws issued by the tribal council which impact news media. As traditionally interpreted, this First Amendment clause is primarily for Native journalists and can be interpreted to mean it is for Nez Perce tribal members only, especially since the Tribal Code (2000) specifically addresses the interest in protecting tribal sovereignty and jurisdiction and the validity of tribal laws; but this has not been challenged by outside interests such as mainstream media.

The Nez Perce Tribal Code (2000, section 1-1-6) also allows for court records, with exceptions, to be open for public inspection. These specific exceptions are: adoptions, incompetency proceedings, juvenile court matters and records sealed by court order. The Tribal Code does allow for non-identified information for "purposes of legitimate research or study upon order of the court as long as such information does not identify or tend to reveal the identity of any individual upon which it is based."

Shoshone-Bannock Tribes

Currently, the tribe has one media outlet, the weekly Sho-Ban News, although the paper is also active on social media such as Facebook and YouTube. In addition, the tribe does use its website to communicate with its members.

In the Shoshone-Bannock tribe's constitution (1936), Article VII, Section 3, Civil Liberties, specifically states that all members of the tribes "may enjoy without hindrance freedom of worship, conscience, speech, press, assembly, and association." Beyond that, the tribes have no additional press freedoms. The constitution speaks specifically to tribal members, as the constitution was designed to protect tribal members and their cultures, and mainstream journalists or members of other tribes are not necessarily privileged to the same rights under tribal law.

Shoshone-Paiute Tribes

Like many tribes, the Shoshone-Paiute constitution has a bill of rights, with the following language: "*Civil liberties.*-All members of the tribes may enjoy without hindrance freedom of worship, conscience, speech, press, assembly, and association." This does not give specific press freedom, but like the First Amendment to the U.S. Constitution it does allow for the right for tribal journalists to publish.

Although the tribal headquarters are physically located in Nevada, the Shoshone-Paiute have a presence in the Duck Valley between Idaho and Nevada. The tribe's Sho-Pai News is a monthly publication which is also accessed online at the tribal website (http://www.shopaitribes.org/spt-15/index.php/). Based in Owyhee, Nevada, the newspaper covers important aspects of tribal life, including irrigation programs and children/youth events.

Northwestern Band of the Shoshone Nation

Much like the civil rights clause in other tribal constitutions, the Northwestern Band of the Shoshone Nation has the wording under Article IX – Rights of Members: "The right to enjoy freedom of worship, conscience, speech, press, assembly and association, and other rights enumerated by the Indian Civil Rights Act of 1968 (25 U.S.C. 1301 et. seq.)." For additional information, see the tribe's website at http://www.nwbshoshone.com/culture/history/NWBSN_Constitution.

Perhaps because the tribe became federally recognized in 1987, the Northern Band of the Shoshone do not have any news outlets, using their website as the primary communications tool. However, the tribe's constitution does allow for freedom of the press.

Kootenai Tribe of Idaho

The Kootenai Tribe does not have a news media outlet, but they do maintain a website for communication (http://kootenai.org). Under the 1947 constitution for the Confederated Salish and Kootenai Tribes of the Flathead Reservation in Montana, tribal members do have four First Amendment freedoms: "All members of the Confederated Tribes may enjoy without hindrance freedom of worship, speech, press, and assembly." The tribe's constitution can be found at http://loc.gov/law/help/american-indian-consts/PDF/36026096.

It should be noted: the Kootenai's constitution is the one filed by the Confederated Salish and Kootenai

Tribes of the Flathead Reservation in Montana; the separate Kootenai Tribe of Idaho did not receive federal recognition until 1975 and had no formal constitution. At that time, the tribe was down to 67 members and the Kootenais were dying out. In 1974, Tribal Chief Amy Tice declared war on the United States to bring attention to the plight of the people (Rosario, 2008). By 2016, the tribe was again thriving with more than 2,000 members, although no news media is yet present.

Working with Tribes

Working with individual tribes does not need to be difficult, but it does require patience. Because of the way tribes have been treated in the past, there is frequently distrust by tribal members toward mainstream news media who may have unfairly or stereotypically portrayed the tribe in the past. The first thing a reporter/editor/producer should do is learn about the tribe – not just local legends but facts which can be gleaned from the tribal website.

Then reporters need to build trust (Tallent, 2013). Reporters should not just parachute in during a breaking news story. They should cultivate a long-term relationship by covering other elements of reservation or tribal life, such as children's sports, care of the elderly, fishing rights issues and other elements important to Native culture. Even just attending events on tribal lands can help build trust, which is key to developing resources.

One thing all journalists and non-tribal members should keep in mind is that the tribes are led by the tribal councils, which have sole authority over the cultures and information released. Each tribal council is very much aware their people, images and cultures have been appropriated in negative ways many times in the past, which have worked against the tribes, therefore most councils are highly suspicious of any outsider. More than anything else, most tribal councils want to protect their people and culture from any more outside invaders who could destroy their traditions and way of life. Caution is always advised and non-Native journalists should be prepared to be rejected when they seek comments while covering a news story.

But if journalists take the Society of Professional Journalists Code of Ethics (1914) seriously, they cannot avoid or ignore these three phrases under the "Seek Truth and Report It" section, where it says journalists should:

- Tell the story of the diversity and magnitude of the human experience boldly, even when it is unpopular to do so.
- Examine their own cultural values and avoid imposing those values on others.
- Avoid stereotyping by race, gender, age, religion, ethnicity, geography, sexual orientation, disability, physical appearance or social status.

This means journalists should not appropriate Native images (such as dressing in Native attire or calling Native Americans "animals" as was suggested by a Minnesota reporter in 2013), using Native symbols for non-Native uses or even calling another person an "Indian-giver" as was done on an exchange between anchors on the Today show (Tallent, 2013).

Native and other groups do not mind genuine inquiry and will help journalists and others to better understand their cultures if they are asked respectfully. It does take some time, but it can be a powerful tool for future stories if reporters and editors will think to check the accuracy of these words and depictions (Tallent, 2013).

References

Brownstein, A.E., McDonald, R.N. & Menikoff, J.A. (case editors). (1977). Equal protection under the Indian Civil Rights Act: *Martinez v. Santa Clara Pueblo. Harvard Law Review. 90*(3) 627-636.

Coeur d'Alene Tribe (1947, Aug. 8). Constitution and by-laws of the Coeur d'Alene Tribe of Idaho. Retrieved from Thorpe Collection, University of Oklahoma at http://thorpe.ou.edu/IRA/coeurcons.html

Confederated Salish and Kootenai Tribes of the Flathead Reservation, Montana. (1935). Constitution and by-laws. Retrieved on July 17, 2016 from the Library of Congress at http://www.loc.gov/law/help/american-indian-consts/PDF/36026096.pdf

Johnson, B.B. (1982, January). "American Indian jurisdiction as a policy issue." *Social Work, the Journal of the National of Social Workers, Inc.* 27 (1) 31-38.

Littlefield, D.F. & Parins, J.W. (1984). *American Indian and Alaska Native newspapers and periodicals*, 1925-1970. New York, NY: Greenwood Press.

Loew, P. & Mella, K. (2005). "Black ink and the real red power: American Indian newspapers and tribal sovereignty." Monograph for the Association for Education in Journalism and Mass Communications.

Marshall, J. (1831). Opinion of the court, C. 30 US 1 Cherokee Nation v. Georgia. Retrieved from Cornell University School of Law archives at http://www.law.cornell.edu/supct/html/historics/USSC_CR_0030_0001_ZO.html

Murphy, S.M. (1998). "Native American media." *History of the mass media in the United States, an encyclopedia.* Pages 420-422. Abingdon, Oxfordshire, United Kingdom: Taylor & Francis, Ltd.

Nez Perce Tribe (2005, May 5-7). Revised constitution and by-laws of the Nez Perce Tribe. Retrieved from the Nez Perce Tribe website on June 30, 2016 from http://www.nezperce.org/Official/PDF/GC/Constitution&ByLaws.pdf

Nez Perce Tribal Code (2000). Retrieved from the Nez Perce Tribe Website on June 30, 2016 from http://www.nezperce.org/~code/pdf%20convert%20files/12jan16%20Code%20with%20TOC%20%20.pdf

News staff (2012, Aug. 12). "Money from federal lawsuit distributed among Sho-Ban members." Local News 8 website retrieved on July 7, 2016 from http://www.localnews8.com/news/Money-from-federal-lawsuit-distributed-among-Sho-Ban-members/16429304

Northwestern Band of the Shoshone Nation (2006). Constitution. Retrieved from the Northwestern band of the Shoshone Nation website on July 17,

2016 at http://www.nwbshoshone.com/culture/history/NWBSN_Constitution

Rosario, S. (Director). (2008). "Idaho's forgotten war" [documentary film]. Meridian, Idaho: Sonya Rosario Productions.

Shoshone-Bannock Tribes (1936, April 30). Constitution and by-laws for the Shoshone-Bannock Tribes of the Fort Hall Reservation, Idaho. Retrieved from the Shoshone-Bannock Tribes website at http://www.shoshonebannocktribes.com/shoshone-bannock-constitution.html

Shoshone-Paiute Constitution (1936). Retrieved from the University of Oklahoma Thorpe Archives on July 17, 2016 at http://thorpe.ou.edu/IRA/duckcons.html

Code of Ethics (2014, Sept. 6). Society of Professional Journalists. Retrieved from http://www.spj.org/ethicscode.asp.

Tallent, R.J. (2013, May/June). "Don't misrepresent Native America." *Quill. 101*(3) 26.

Tallent, R.J. (2012, July/Aug). "Shields up in Indian country." *Quill. 100*(4) 34-36.

Tallent, R.J. & Dingman, R.S. (2011). "Native press freedoms: Federal and tribal legal issues restricting native media." Chapter in *Interracial communication: Contexts, communities, and choices*. Brunson, D.A., Lampl, L.L. & Jordan-Jackson, F.F. (eds). Dubuque, IA: Kendall Hunt Publishing Co.

Appendix A

TITLE 74

Transparent and Ethical Government

Chapter 1

Public Records Act

74-105. RECORDS EXEMPT FROM DISCLOSURE -- LAW ENFORCEMENT RECORDS, INVESTIGATORY RECORDS OF AGENCIES, EVACUATION AND EMERGENCY RESPONSE PLANS, WORKER'S COMPENSATION. The following records are exempt from disclosure:

(1) Investigatory records of a law enforcement agency, as defined in section 74-101 (7), Idaho Code, under the conditions set forth in section 74-124, Idaho Code.

(2) Juvenile records of a person maintained pursuant to chapter 5, title 20, Idaho Code, except that facts contained in such records shall be furnished upon request in a manner determined by the court to persons and governmental and private agencies and institutions conducting pertinent research studies or having a legitimate interest in the protection, welfare and treatment of the juvenile who is thirteen (13) years of age or younger. If the juvenile is petitioned or charged with an offense which would be a criminal offense if committed by an adult, the name, offense of which the juvenile was petitioned or charged and disposition of the court shall be subject to disclosure as provided in section 20-525, Idaho Code. Additionally,

facts contained in any records of a juvenile maintained under chapter 5, title 20, Idaho Code, shall be furnished upon request to any school district where the juvenile is enrolled or is seeking enrollment.

(3) Records of the custody review board of the Idaho department of juvenile corrections, including records containing the names, addresses and written statements of victims and family members of juveniles, shall be exempt from public disclosure pursuant to section 20-533A, Idaho Code.

(4) (a) The following records of the department of correction:

(i) Records of which the public interest in confidentiality, public safety, security and habilitation clearly outweighs the public interest in disclosure as identified pursuant to the authority of the Idaho board of correction under section 20-212, Idaho Code;

(ii) Records that contain any identifying information, or any information that would lead to the identification of any victims or witnesses;

(iii) Records that reflect future transportation or movement of a prisoner;

(iv) Records gathered during the course of the presentence investigation;

(v) Records of a prisoner, as defined in section 74-101(10), Idaho Code, or probationer shall not be disclosed to any other prisoner or probationer.

(b) Records, other than public expenditure records, related to proposed or existing critical infrastructure held by or in the custody of any public agency only when the disclosure of such information is reasonably likely to jeopardize the safety of persons, property or the public safety. Such records may include emergency evacuation, escape or other emergency response plans, vulnerability assessments, operation and security manuals, plans, blueprints or security codes. For purposes of this section "system" includes electrical, computer and telecommunication systems, electric power, (including production, generating, transportation, transmission and distribution), heating, ventilation, and air conditioning. For purposes of this subsection, "critical infrastructure" means any system or asset, whether physical or virtual, so vital to the state of Idaho, including its political subdivisions, that the incapacity or destruction of such system or asset would have a debilitating impact on state or national economic security, state or national public health or safety or any combination of those matters.

(c) Records of the commission of pardons and parole shall be exempt from public disclosure pursuant to section 20-213A, Idaho Code, and section 20-223, Idaho Code. Records exempt from disclosure shall also include those containing the names, addresses and written statements of victims.

(5) Voting records of the sexual offender classification board. The written record of the vote to classify an offender as a violent sexual predator by each board member in each case reviewed by that board member shall be exempt from disclosure to the public and shall be made available upon request only to the governor, the chairman of the senate judiciary and rules committee, and the chairman of the house of representatives judiciary, rules and administration committee, for all lawful purposes.

(6) Records of the sheriff or Idaho state police received or maintained pursuant to sections 18-3302, 18-

3302H and 18-3302K, Idaho Code, relating to an applicant or licensee except that any law enforcement officer and law enforcement agency, whether inside or outside the state of Idaho, may access information maintained in the license record system as set forth in section 18-3302K (16), Idaho Code.

(7) Records of investigations prepared by the department of health and welfare pursuant to its statutory responsibilities dealing with the protection of children, the rehabilitation of youth, adoptions and the commitment of mentally ill persons. For reasons of health and safety, best interests of the child or public interest, the department of health and welfare may provide for the disclosure of records of investigations associated with actions pursuant to the provisions of chapter 16, title 16, Idaho Code, prepared by the department of health and welfare pursuant to its statutory responsibilities dealing with the protection of children except any such records regarding adoptions shall remain exempt from disclosure.

(8) Records including, but not limited to, investigative reports, resulting from investigations conducted into complaints of discrimination made to the Idaho human rights commission unless the public interest in allowing inspection and copying of such records outweighs the legitimate public or private interest in maintaining confidentiality of such records. A person may inspect and copy documents from an investigative file to which he or she is a named party if such documents are not otherwise prohibited from disclosure by federal law or regulation or state law. The confidentiality of this subsection will no longer apply to any record used in any judicial proceeding brought by a named party to the complaint or investigation, or by the Idaho human rights commission, relating to the complaint of discrimination.

(9) Records containing information obtained by the manager of the Idaho state insurance fund pursuant to chapter 9, title 72, Idaho Code, from or on behalf of employers or employees contained in underwriting and claims for benefits files.

(10) The worker's compensation records of the Idaho industrial commission provided that the industrial commission shall make such records available:

(a) To the parties in any worker's compensation claim and to the industrial special indemnity fund of the state of Idaho; or

(b) To employers and prospective employers subject to the provisions of the Americans with disabilities act, 42 U.S.C. 12112, or other statutory limitations, who certify that the information is being requested with respect to a worker to whom the employer has extended an offer of employment and will be used in accordance with the provisions of the Americans with disabilities act, 42 U.S.C. 12112, or other statutory limitations; or

(c) To employers and prospective employers not subject to the provisions of the Americans with disabilities act, 42 U.S.C. 12112, or other statutory limitations, provided the employer presents a written authorization from the person to whom the records pertain; or

(d) To others who demonstrate that the public interest in allowing inspection and copying of such records outweighs the public or private interest in maintaining the confidentiality of such records, as determined by a civil court of competent jurisdiction; or

(e) Although a claimant's records maintained by the industrial commission, including medical and rehabilitation records, are otherwise exempt from public disclosure, the quoting or discussing of medical or rehabilitation records contained in the industrial commission's records during a hearing for compensation or in a written decision issued by the industrial commission shall be permitted; provided further, the true identification of the parties shall not be exempt from public disclosure in any written decision issued and released to the public by the industrial commission.

(11) Records of investigations compiled by the commission on aging involving vulnerable adults, as defined in section 18-1505, Idaho Code, alleged to be abused, neglected or exploited.

(12) Criminal history records and fingerprints, as defined by section67-3001, Idaho Code, and compiled by the Idaho state police. Such records shall be released only in accordance with chapter 30, title 67, Idaho Code.

(13) Records furnished or obtained pursuant to section 41-1019, Idaho Code, regarding termination of an appointment, employment, contract or other insurance business relationship between an insurer and a producer.

(14) Records of a prisoner or former prisoner in the custody of any state or local correctional facility, when the request is made by another prisoner in the custody of any state or local correctional facility.

(15) Except as provided in section 72-1007, Idaho Code, records of the Idaho industrial commission relating to compensation for crime victims under chapter 10, title 72, Idaho Code.

(16) Records or information identifying a complainant maintained by the department of health and welfare pursuant to section 39-3556, Idaho Code, relating to certified family homes, unless the complainant consents in writing to the disclosure or the disclosure of the com-

plainant's identity is required in any administrative or judicial proceeding.

(17) Records of any certification or notification required by federal law to be made in connection with the acquisition or transfer of a firearm, including a firearm as defined in 26 U.S.C. 5845(a).

History:

[74-105, added 2015, ch. 140, sec. 5, p. 349; am. 2015, ch. 303, sec. 8, p. 1199; am. 2016, ch. 164, sec. 1, p. 446; am. 2016, ch. 279, sec. 1, p. 769.]

Title 74

Transparent and Ethical Government

Chapter 1

Public Records Act

74-106. RECORDS EXEMPT FROM DISCLOSURE -- PERSONNEL RECORDS, PERSONAL INFORMATION, HEALTH RECORDS, PROFESSIONAL DISCIPLINE. The following records are exempt from disclosure:

(1) Except as provided in this subsection, all personnel records of a current or former public official other than the public official's public service or employment history, classification, pay grade and step, longevity, gross salary and salary history, status, workplace and employing agency. All other personnel information relating to a public employee or applicant including, but not limited to, information regarding sex, race, marital status, birth date, home address and telephone number, applications, testing and scoring materials, grievances, correspondence

and performance evaluations, shall not be disclosed to the public without the employee's or applicant's written consent. Names of applicants to classified or merit system positions shall not be disclosed to the public without the applicant's written consent. Disclosure of names as part of a background check is permitted. Names of the five (5) final applicants to all other positions shall be available to the public. If such group is less than five (5) finalists, then the entire list of applicants shall be available to the public. A public official or authorized representative may inspect and copy his personnel records, except for material used to screen and test for employment.

(2) Retired employees' and retired public officials' home addresses, home telephone numbers and other financial and nonfinancial membership records; active and inactive member financial and membership records and mortgage portfolio loan documents maintained by the public employee retirement system. Financial statements prepared by retirement system staff, funding agents and custodians concerning the investment of assets of the public employee retirement system of Idaho are not considered confidential under this chapter.

(3) Information and records submitted to the Idaho state lottery for the performance of background investigations of employees, lottery retailers and major procurement contractors; audit records of lottery retailers, vendors and major procurement contractors submitted to or performed by the Idaho state lottery; validation and security tests of the state lottery for lottery games; business records and information submitted pursuant to sections 67-7412(8) and (9) and 67-7421(8) and (9), Idaho Code, and such documents and information obtained and held for the purposes of lottery security and investigative action as determined by lottery rules unless the public

interest in disclosure substantially outweighs the private need for protection from public disclosure.

(4) Records of a personal nature as follows:

(a) Records of personal debt filed with a public agency or independent public body corporate and politic pursuant to law;

(b) Personal bank records compiled by a public depositor for the purpose of public funds transactions conducted pursuant to law;

(c) Records of ownership of financial obligations and instruments of a public agency or independent public body corporate and politic, such as bonds, compiled by the public agency or independent public body corporate and politic pursuant to law;

(d) Records, with regard to the ownership of, or security interests in, registered public obligations;

(e) Vital statistics records; and

(f) Military records as described in and pursuant to section 65-301, Idaho Code.

(5) Information in an income or other tax return measured by items of income or sales, which is gathered by a public agency for the purpose of administering the tax, except such information to the extent disclosed in a written decision of the tax commission pursuant to a taxpayer protest of a deficiency determination by the tax commission, under the provisions of section 63-3045B, Idaho Code.

(6) Records of a personal nature related directly or indirectly to the application for and provision of statutory services rendered to persons applying for public care for people who are elderly, indigent or have mental or physical disabilities, or participation in an environmental or a public health study, provided the provisions of this subsection making records exempt from disclosure shall

not apply to the extent that such records or information contained in those records are necessary for a background check on an individual that is required by federal law regulating the sale of firearms, guns or ammunition.

(7) Employment security information, except that a person may agree, through written, informed consent, to waive the exemption so that a third party may obtain information pertaining to the person, unless access to the information by the person is restricted by subsection (3)(a), (3)(b) or (3)(d) of section 74-113, Idaho Code. Notwithstanding the provisions of section 74-113, Idaho Code, a person may not review identifying information concerning an informant who reported to the department of labor a suspected violation by the person of the employment security law, chapter 13, title 72, Idaho Code, under an assurance of confidentiality. As used in this section and in chapter 13, title 72, Idaho Code, "employment security information" means any information descriptive of an identifiable person or persons that is received by, recorded by, prepared by, furnished to or collected by the department of labor or the industrial commission in the administration of the employment security law.

(8) Any personal records, other than names, business addresses and business phone numbers, such as parentage, race, religion, sex, height, weight, tax identification and social security numbers, financial worth or medical condition submitted to any public agency or independent public body corporate and politic pursuant to a statutory requirement for licensing, certification, permit or bonding.

(9) Unless otherwise provided by agency rule, information obtained as part of an inquiry into a person's fitness to be granted or retain a license, certificate, permit, privilege, commission or position, private association

peer review committee records authorized in title 54, Idaho Code. Any agency which has records exempt from disclosure under the provisions of this subsection shall annually make available a statistical summary of the number and types of matters considered and their disposition.

(10) The records, findings, determinations and decisions of any prelitigation screening panel formed under chapters 10 and 23, title 6, Idaho Code.

(11) Complaints received by the board of medicine and investigations and informal proceedings, including informal proceedings of any committee of the board of medicine, pursuant to chapter 18, title 54, Idaho Code, and rules adopted thereunder.

(12) Records of the department of health and welfare or a public health district that identify a person infected with a reportable disease.

(13) Records of hospital care, medical records, including prescriptions, drug orders, records or any other prescription information that specifically identifies an individual patient, prescription records maintained by the board of pharmacy under sections 37-2726 and 37-2730A, Idaho Code, records of psychiatric care or treatment and professional counseling records relating to an individual's condition, diagnosis, care or treatment, provided the provisions of this subsection making records exempt from disclosure shall not apply to the extent that such records or information contained in those records are necessary for a background check on an individual that is required by federal law regulating the sale of firearms, guns or ammunition.

(14) Information collected pursuant to the directory of new hires act, chapter 16, title 72, Idaho Code.

(15) Personal information contained in motor vehicle

and driver records that is exempt from disclosure under the provisions of chapter 2, title 49, Idaho Code.

(16) Records of the financial status of prisoners pursuant to subsection (2) of section 20-607, Idaho Code.

(17) Records of the Idaho state police or department of correction received or maintained pursuant to section 19-5514, Idaho Code, relating to DNA databases and databanks.

(18) Records of the department of health and welfare relating to a survey, resurvey or complaint investigation of a licensed nursing facility shall be exempt from disclosure. Such records shall, however, be subject to disclosure as public records as soon as the facility in question has received the report, and no later than the fourteenth day following the date that department of health and welfare representatives officially exit the facility pursuant to federal regulations. Provided however, that for purposes of confidentiality, no record shall be released under this section which specifically identifies any nursing facility resident.

(19) Records and information contained in the registry of immunizations against childhood diseases maintained in the department of health and welfare, including information disseminated to others from the registry by the department of health and welfare.

(20) Records of the Idaho housing and finance association (IHFA) relating to the following:

(a) Records containing personal financial, family, health or similar personal information submitted to or otherwise obtained by the IHFA;

(b) Records submitted to or otherwise obtained by the IHFA with regard to obtaining and servicing mortgage loans and all records relating to the review, approval or rejection by the IHFA of said loans;

(c) Mortgage portfolio loan documents;

(d) Records of a current or former employee other than the employee's duration of employment with the association, position held and location of employment. This exemption from disclosure does not include the contracts of employment or any remuneration, including reimbursement of expenses, of the executive director, executive officers or commissioners of the association. All other personnel information relating to an association employee or applicant including, but not limited to, information regarding sex, race, marital status, birth date, home address and telephone number, applications, testing and scoring materials, grievances, correspondence, retirement plan information and performance evaluations, shall not be disclosed to the public without the employee's or applicant's written consent. An employee or authorized representative may inspect and copy that employee's personnel records, except for material used to screen and test for employment or material not subject to disclosure elsewhere in the Idaho public records act.

(21) Records of the department of health and welfare related to child support services in cases in which there is reasonable evidence of domestic violence, as defined in chapter 63, title 39, Idaho Code, that can be used to locate any individuals in the child support case except in response to a court order.

(22) Records of the Idaho state bar lawyer assistance program pursuant to chapter 49, title 54, Idaho Code, unless a participant in the program authorizes the release pursuant to subsection (4) of section 54-4901, Idaho Code.

(23) Records and information contained in the trauma

registry created by chapter 20, title 57, Idaho Code, together with any reports, analyses and compilations created from such information and records.

(24) Records contained in the court files, or other records prepared as part of proceedings for judicial authorization of sterilization procedures pursuant to chapter 39, title 39, Idaho Code.

(25) The physical voter registration application on file in the county clerk's office; however, a redacted copy of said application shall be made available consistent with the requirements of this section. Information from the voter registration application maintained in the statewide voter registration database, including age, will be made available except for the voter's driver's license number, date of birth and, upon a showing that the voter comes within the provisions of subsection (30) of this section or upon showing of good cause by the voter to the county clerk in consultation with the county prosecuting attorney, the physical residence address of the voter. For the purposes of this subsection good cause shall include the protection of life and property and protection of victims of domestic violence and similar crimes.

(26) File numbers, passwords and information in the files of the health care directive registry maintained by the secretary of state under section 39-4515, Idaho Code, are confidential and shall not be disclosed to any person other than to the person who executed the health care directive or the revocation thereof and that person's legal representatives, to the person who registered the health care directive or revocation thereof, and to physicians, hospitals, medical personnel, nursing homes, and other persons who have been granted file number and password access to the documents within that specific file.

(27) Records in an address confidentiality program

participant's file as provided for in chapter 57, title 19, Idaho Code, other than the address designated by the secretary of state, except under the following circumstances:

(a) If requested by a law enforcement agency, to the law enforcement agency; or

(b) If directed by a court order, to a person identified in the order.

(28) Except as otherwise provided by law relating to the release of information to a governmental entity or law enforcement agency, any personal information including, but not limited to, names, personal and business addresses and phone numbers, sex, height, weight, date of birth, social security and driver's license numbers, or any other identifying numbers and/or information related to any Idaho fish and game licenses, permits and tags unless written consent is obtained from the affected person.

(29) Documents and records related to alternatives to discipline that are maintained by the Idaho board of veterinary medicine under the provisions of section 54-2118(1)(b), Idaho Code, provided the requirements set forth therein are met.

(30) The Idaho residential street address and telephone number of an eligible law enforcement officer and such officer's residing household member(s) as provided for in chapter 58, title 19, Idaho Code, except under the following circumstances:

(a) If directed by a court order, to a person identified in the court order;

(b) If requested by a law enforcement agency, to the law enforcement agency;

(c) If requested by a financial institution or title company for business purposes, to the requesting financial institution or title company; or

(d) If the law enforcement officer provides written permission for disclosure of such information.

(31) All information exchanged between the Idaho transportation department and insurance companies, any database created, all information contained in the verification system and all reports, responses or other information generated for the purposes of the verification system, pursuant to section 49-1234, Idaho Code.

(32) Nothing in this section shall prohibit the release of information to the state controller as the state social security administrator as provided in section 59-1101A, Idaho Code.

(33) Personal information including, but not limited to, property values, personal and business addresses, phone numbers, dates of birth, social security and driver's license numbers or any other identifying numbers or information maintained by the administrator of the unclaimed property law set forth in chapter 5, title 14, Idaho Code. Nothing in this subsection shall prohibit the release of names, last known city of residence, property value ranges and general property information by the administrator for the purpose of reuniting unclaimed property with its owner.

History:

[74-106, added 2015, ch. 140, sec. 5, p. 351; am. 2016, ch. 343, sec. 2, p. 982; am. 2016, ch. 359, sec. 9, p. 1056.]

Title 74

Transparent and Ethical Government

Chapter 1

Public Records Act

74-107. RECORDS EXEMPT FROM DISCLOSURE -- TRADE SECRETS, PRODUCTION RECORDS, APPRAISALS, BIDS, PROPRIETARY INFORMATION. The following records are exempt from disclosure:

(1) Trade secrets including those contained in response to public agency or independent public body corporate and politic requests for proposal, requests for clarification, requests for information and similar requests. "Trade secrets" as used in this section means information, including a formula, pattern, compilation, program, computer program, device, method, technique, process, or unpublished or in-progress research that:

(a) Derives independent economic value, actual or potential, from not being generally known to, and not being readily ascertainable by proper means by other persons who can obtain economic value from its disclosure or use; and

(b) Is the subject of efforts that are reasonable under the circumstances to maintain its secrecy.

(2) Production records, housing production, rental and financing records, sale or purchase records, catch records, mortgage portfolio loan documents, or similar business records of a private concern or enterprise required by law to be submitted to or inspected by a public agency or submitted to or otherwise obtained by an independent public body corporate and politic. Nothing in this subsection shall limit the use which can be made

of such information for regulatory purposes or its admissibility in any enforcement proceeding.

(3) Records relating to the appraisal of real property, timber or mineral rights prior to its acquisition, sale or lease by a public agency or independent public body corporate and politic.

(4) Any estimate prepared by a public agency or independent public body corporate and politic that details the cost of a public project until such time as disclosed or bids are opened, or upon award of the contract for construction of the public project.

(5) Examination, operating or condition reports and all documents relating thereto, prepared by or supplied to any public agency or independent public body corporate and politic responsible for the regulation or supervision of financial institutions including, but not limited to, banks, savings and loan associations, regulated lenders, business and industrial development corporations, credit unions, and insurance companies, or for the regulation or supervision of the issuance of securities.

(6) Records gathered by a local agency or the Idaho department of commerce, as described in chapter 47, title 67, Idaho Code, for the specific purpose of assisting a person to locate, maintain, invest in, or expand business operations in the state of Idaho.

(7) Shipping and marketing records of commodity commissions used to evaluate marketing and advertising strategies and the names and addresses of growers and shippers maintained by commodity commissions.

(8) Financial statements and business information and reports submitted by a legal entity to a port district organized under title 70, Idaho Code, in connection with a business agreement, or with a development proposal

or with a financing application for any industrial, manufacturing, or other business activity within a port district.

(9) Names and addresses of seed companies, seed crop growers, seed crop consignees, locations of seed crop fields, variety name and acreage by variety. Upon the request of the owner of the proprietary variety, this information shall be released to the owner. Provided however, that if a seed crop has been identified as diseased or has been otherwise identified by the Idaho department of agriculture, other state departments of agriculture, or the United States department of agriculture to represent a threat to that particular seed or commercial crop industry or to individual growers, information as to test results, location, acreage involved and disease symptoms of that particular seed crop, for that growing season, shall be available for public inspection and copying. This exemption shall not supersede the provisions of section 22-436, Idaho Code, nor shall this exemption apply to information regarding specific property locations subject to an open burning of crop residue pursuant to section 39-114, Idaho Code, names of persons responsible for the open burn, acreage and crop type to be burned, and time frames for burning.

(10) Information obtained from books, records and accounts required in chapter 47, title 22, Idaho Code, to be maintained by the Idaho oilseed commission and pertaining to the individual production records of oilseed growers.

(11) Records of any risk retention or self-insurance program prepared in anticipation of litigation or for analysis of or settlement of potential or actual money damage claims against a public entity and its employees or against the industrial special indemnity fund except as otherwise discoverable under the Idaho or federal rules

of civil procedure. These records shall include, but are not limited to, claims evaluations, investigatory records, computerized reports of losses, case reserves, internal documents and correspondence relating thereto. At the time any claim is concluded, only statistical data and actual amounts paid in settlement shall be deemed a public record unless otherwise ordered to be sealed by a court of competent jurisdiction. Provided however, nothing in this subsection is intended to limit the attorney client privilege or attorney work product privilege otherwise available to any public agency or independent public body corporate and politic.

(12) Records of laboratory test results provided by or retained by the Idaho food quality assurance laboratory. Nothing in this subsection shall limit the use which can be made, or availability of such information if used, for regulatory purposes or its admissibility in any enforcement proceeding.

(13) Reports required to be filed under chapter 13, title 62, Idaho Code, identifying electrical or natural or manufactured gas consumption data for an individual customer or account.

(14) Voluntarily prepared environmental audits, and voluntary disclosures of information submitted on or before December 31, 1997, to an environmental agency, which are claimed to be confidential business information.

(15) Computer programs developed or purchased by or for any public agency or independent public body corporate and politic for its own use. As used in this subsection, "computer program" means a series of instructions or statements which permit the functioning of a computer system in a manner designed to provide storage, retrieval and manipulation of data from the computer system, and

any associated documentation and source material that explain how to operate the computer program. Computer program does not include:

(a) The original data including, but not limited to, numbers, text, voice, graphics and images;

(b) Analysis, compilation and other manipulated forms of the original data produced by use of the program; or

(c) The mathematical or statistical formulas that would be used if the manipulated forms of the original data were to be produced manually.

(16) Active investigative records and trademark usage audits of the Idaho potato commission specifically relating to the enforcement of chapter 12, title 22, Idaho Code, until the commencement of formal proceedings as provided by rules of the commission; purchase and sales information submitted to the Idaho potato commission during a trademark usage audit, and investigation or enforcement proceedings. Inactive investigatory records shall be disclosed unless the disclosure would violate the standards set forth in subsection (1)(a) through (f) of section 74-124, Idaho Code. Nothing in this subsection shall limit the use which can be made, or availability of such information if used, for regulatory purposes or its admissibility in any enforcement proceeding.

(17) All records copied or obtained by the director of the department of agriculture or his designee as a result of an inspection pursuant to section 25-3806, Idaho Code, except:

(a) Records otherwise deemed to be public records not exempt from disclosure pursuant to this chapter; and

(b) Inspection reports, determinations of compliance or noncompliance and all other records created by the director or his designee pursuant to section 25-3806, Idaho Code.

(18) All data and information collected by the division of animal industries or the state brand board pursuant to the provisions of section 25-207B, Idaho Code, or rules promulgated thereunder.

(19) Records disclosed to a county official by the state tax commission pursuant to subsection (4)(c) of section 63-3029B, Idaho Code.

(20) Records, data, information and materials collected, developed, generated, ascertained or discovered during the course of academic research at public institutions of higher education if the disclosure of such could reasonably affect the conduct or outcome of the research, or the ability of the public institution of higher education to patent or copyright the research or protect intellectual property.

(21) Records, data, information and materials collected or utilized during the course of academic research at public institutions of higher education provided by any person or entity other than the public institution of higher education or a public agency.

(22) The exemptions from disclosure provided in subsections (20) and (21) of this section shall apply only until the academic research is publicly released, copyrighted or patented, or until the academic research is completed or terminated. At such time, the records, data, information, and materials shall be subject to public disclosure unless: (a) another exemption in this chapter applies; (b) such information was provided to the institution subject to a written agreement of confidentiality; or (c) public disclosure would pose a danger to persons or property.

(23) The exemptions from disclosure provided in subsections (20) and (21) of this section do not include

basic information about a particular research project that is otherwise subject to public disclosure, such as the nature of the academic research, the name of the researcher, and the amount and source of the funding provided for the project.

(24) Records of a county assessor, the state tax commission, a county board of equalization or the state board of tax appeals containing the following information: (i) lists of personal property required to be filed pursuant to section 63-302, Idaho Code, and operating statements required to be filed pursuant to section 63-404, Idaho Code, and (ii) confidential commercial or financial information including trade secrets. Except with respect to lists of personal property required to be filed pursuant to section 63-302, Idaho Code, and the operator statements required to be filed pursuant to section 63-404, Idaho Code, it shall be the responsibility of the taxpayer to give notice of its claim to exemption by stamping or marking each page or the first page of each portion of documents so claimed. No records that are exempt pursuant to this subsection shall be disclosed without the consent of the taxpayer except as follows:

(a) To any officer, employee or authorized representative of the state or the United States, under a continuing claim of confidentiality, as necessary to carry out the provisions of state or federal law or when relevant to any proceeding thereunder.

(b) In the publication of statistics or reports as long as the statistics or reports do not reasonably lead to the identification of the specific taxpayer or information submitted by taxpayers exempt pursuant to this subsection.

(c) To the board of tax appeals or the district court as evidence or otherwise in connection with an appeal of the taxpayer's property tax assessment, but only if the board or the court, as applicable, has entered a protective order specifying that the taxpayer information may not be disclosed by any person conducting or participating in the action or proceeding, except as authorized by the board or the court in accordance with applicable law.

(d) Nothing in this subsection shall prevent disclosure of the following information:

(i) Name and mailing address of the property owner;

(ii) A parcel number;

(iii) A legal description of real property;

(iv) The square footage and acreage of real property;

(v) The assessed value of taxable property;

(vi) The tax district and the tax rate; and

(vii) The total property tax assessed.

(25) Results of laboratory tests which have no known adverse impacts to human health conducted by the Idaho state department of agriculture animal health laboratory, related to diagnosis of animal diseases of individual animals or herds, on samples submitted by veterinarians or animal owners unless:

(a) The laboratory test results indicate the presence of a state or federally reportable or regulated disease in animals;

(b) The release of the test results is required by state or federal law; or

(c) The test result is identified as representing a threat to animal or human health or to the livestock industry by the Idaho state department of agriculture or the United States department of agriculture. Nothing in this subsection shall limit the use which can be made, or availability of such information if used, for regulatory purposes or its admissibility in any enforcement proceeding, or the duty of any person to report contagious or infectious diseases as required by state or federal law.

(26) Results of laboratory tests conducted by the Idaho state department of agriculture seed laboratory on samples submitted by seed producers or seed companies. Nothing in this subsection shall limit the use which can be made, or availability of such information pursuant to the provisions of subsections (9) and (10) of section 22-418, Idaho Code.

(27) For policies that are owned by private persons, and not by a public agency of the state of Idaho, records of policies, endorsements, affidavits and any records that discuss policies, endorsements and affidavits that may be required to be filed with or by a surplus line association pursuant to chapter 12, title 41, Idaho Code.

(28) Individual financial statements of a postsecondary educational institution or a proprietary school submitted to the state board of education, its director or a representative thereof, for the purpose of registering the postsecondary educational institution or proprietary school pursuant to section 33-2402 or 33-2403, Idaho Code, or provided pursuant to an administrative rule of the board adopted pursuant to such sections.

(29) Information submitted to [by] insurance companies pursuant to section 42[41]-612(17), Idaho Code.

History:

[74-107, added 2015, ch. 140, sec. 5, p. 355; am. 2016, ch. 68, sec. 3, p. 237.]

Title 74

Transparent and Ethical Government

Chapter 1

Public Records Act

74-114. ACCESS TO AIR QUALITY, WATER QUALITY AND HAZARDOUS WASTE RECORDS -- PROTECTION OF TRADE SECRETS. (1) To the extent required by the federal clean air act, the federal clean water act and the resource conservation and recovery act for state primacy over any delegated or authorized programs, even if the record is otherwise exempt from disclosure under this chapter, any person may inspect and copy:

(a) Air pollution emission data;

(b) The content of any title V operating permit;

(c) The name and address of any Idaho pollutant discharge elimination system (IPDES) applicant or permittee;

(d) The content of any IPDES permit;

(e) IPDES permit applications, and information required to be submitted by IPDES application forms, whether the information is submitted on the application forms themselves or in any attachments used to supply information required by the application forms;

(f) Effluent data or a standard or limitation, as defined in 40 CFR 2.302;

(g) The name and address of any applicant or permittee for a hazardous waste treatment, storage, or disposal facility permit pursuant to chapter 44, title 39, Idaho Code; and

(h) Any other record required to be provided to

or obtained by the department of environmental quality pursuant to the federal clean air act, the federal clean water act and the resource conservation and recovery act, and the implementing state statutes, federal regulations and state rules, unless the record is a trade secret.

(2) For purposes of this section, a record, or a portion of the record, is a "trade secret" if the information contained in the record is a trade secret within the meaning of the Idaho trade secrets act, sections 48-801, et seq., Idaho Code, including commercial or financial information which, if disclosed, could cause substantial competitive harm to the person from whom the record was obtained.

(3) Any record, or portion of a record, provided to or obtained by the department of environmental quality and identified by the person providing the record as a trade secret shall not be disclosed to the public and shall be kept confidential according to the procedures established in this section.

(4) Nothing in this section shall be construed as limiting the disclosure of a trade secret by the department of environmental quality:

(a) To any officer, employee, or authorized representative of the state or the United States, under a continuing claim of confidentiality, as necessary to carry out the provisions of state or federal law, or when relevant to any proceeding thereunder;

(b) As determined necessary by the director of the department of environmental quality (under a continuing confidentiality claim) to protect the public health and safety from imminent and substantial endangerment;

(c) As required by state or federal law, including section 74-115(3), Idaho Code, under a continuing claim of confidentiality and subsection (1) of this section; or

(d) With the consent of the person from whom the record is obtained.

(5) It shall be the responsibility of any person providing a record to the department of environmental quality to give notice of the existence of a trade secret on each page or other portion of information at the time of submittal, and such person shall have the burden of demonstrating that the information is a trade secret.

(6) Notwithstanding the time frames set forth in section 74-103(1), Idaho Code, when a request is made to the department of environmental quality pursuant to the provisions of this chapter for the disclosure of information for which a trade secret claim has been made, and the information has not been demonstrated to be a trade secret to the satisfaction of the director of the department of environmental quality, within three (3) working days of receipt of the request for the disclosure of the information, the department of environmental quality shall provide a written request for substantiation to the person making the confidentiality claim. A response shall be submitted to the department of environmental quality by the person claiming the trade secret protection within ten (10) working days after receipt of the request for substantiation, or the information subject to the claim shall be disclosed without further notice. Upon receipt of a timely response to the request for substantiation, the director of the department of environmental quality shall determine whether the information is a trade secret subject to protection.

(a) If it is determined that the information, or any portion of the information, is a trade secret, within three (3) working days after receipt of the response, the director of the department of environmental quality shall notify the person requesting the information that the request is denied pursuant to subsections (3) and (4) of section 74-103, Idaho Code.

(b) If it is determined that the information, or any portion of the information, is not a trade secret and is, therefore, subject to disclosure, within three (3) working days after receipt of the response, the director of the department of environmental quality shall inform the person making the confidentiality claim of the determination. The decision shall be a final agency action directly appealable, de novo, to the district court of the county where the records or some part thereof are located. An appeal contesting the decision of the director of the department of environmental quality to release information claimed to be a trade secret shall be filed within ten (10) working days from the date of receipt of the written notice of decision. The information claimed to be a trade secret shall not be disclosed until the period for appeal has expired with no appeal being taken, or a court order has been issued finding that the information is not a trade secret and all appeals of that order have been exhausted.

(7) In any appeal taken pursuant to this section, the court may award reasonable costs and attorney's fees to the prevailing party if it finds the claim of confidentiality or the decision of the director of the department of environmental quality to provide records was frivolously pursued.

(8) The department of environmental quality shall adopt rules which include:

(a) Appropriate measures to safeguard and protect against improper disclosure of trade secrets, including procedures to train all employees on the proper handling of trade secrets; and

(b) Any other provisions necessary to carry out this section.

(9) As it relates to the department of environmental quality, or to agents, contractors, or other representatives of the department, the immunity created in section 74-118, Idaho Code, shall apply only when disclosure of a trade secret is made consistent with this section.

History:

[74-114, added 2015, ch. 140, sec. 5, p. 362; am. 2016, ch. 146, sec. 1, p. 413.]

Appendix B

Chapter 2

Open Meetings Law

74-206A. NEGOTIATIONS IN OPEN SESSION. [EFFECTIVE UNTIL JULY 1, 2020] (1) All negotiations between a governing body and a labor organization shall be in open session and shall be available for the public to attend. This requirement also applies to negotiations between the governing body's designated representatives and representatives of the labor organization. This requirement shall also apply to meetings with any labor negotiation arbitrators, mediators or similar labor dispute meeting facilitators. Provided, however, a governing body or its designated representatives may hold an executive session for the specific purpose of:

(a) Considering a labor contract offer or to formulate a counteroffer; or

(b) Receiving information about a specific employee, when the information has a direct bearing on the issues being negotiated and a reasonable person would conclude that the release of that information would violate that employee's right to privacy.

(2) All documentation exchanged between the parties during negotiations, including all offers, counteroffers and meeting minutes, shall be subject to public writings disclosure laws.

(3) Any other provision of law notwithstanding, including any other provisions to the contrary in sec-

tions 33-402 and 74-204, Idaho Code, the governing body shall post notice of all negotiation sessions at the earliest possible time practicable. This shall be done by the governing body by immediately posting notice of the negotiation session on the front page of its official website. If time permits, the governing body shall also post notice within twenty-four (24) hours at its regular meeting physical posting locations.

(4) Public testimony, if any, shall be posted as an agenda item.

History:

[(74-206A) 67-2345A, added 2015, ch. 271, sec. 2, p. 1126; am. and redesig. 2016, ch. 47, sec. 41, p.125.]

Biographies of Authors and Editors

Justin Barnes, Ph.D., brings teaching experience from the University of Idaho and Washington State University, having developed several courses at each institution. Before joining the faculty, Justin was a clinical assistant professor in the sport management program at WSU. Justin also has industrial experience in New York City with Ruder Finn, Inc., where he assisted clients in public relations, advertising, branding and integrated marketing campaigns. In his final year at RF, Justin researched branding, advertising and integrated marketing trends within social media. In addition to teaching advertising classes, he also advises the competitive UI Advertising Team.

Katie Blevins, Ph.D., received her Ph.D. from the Pennsylvania State University. Prior to arriving at the University of Idaho she spent four years as a Visiting Assistant Professor of Communications at Trinity University in San Antonio, Texas. Her teaching focuses on media law, issues of gender and representation, and other critical/cultural areas of interest. Her research looks at news coverage of legal issues that impact women. At UI she teaches Media Law, Critical Issues (Social Media & Social Change) and Social Media Law in the College of Law.

Susan Dente Ross, Ph.D., is committed to the advancement of social justice and peace and believes that the careful telling of our lives provides fertile ground for compassion, connection, and cooperation. Her profoundly interdisciplinary work draws upon graduate training in journalism, international mass media, law, public policy, and economics, as well as deep and continuing reading in cultural studies, social movements, and peace studies. A Fulbright Scholar and the 2008-'09 University of Calgary Research Fellow in Peace Studies, she has been a Visiting fellow in Greece, Israel and North Cyprus. Her teaching, research, and writing are also informed by life experience as a vocational rehabilitation instructor, a reporter, and a small-town newspaper owner.

Shaakirrah Sanders, J.D., has taught Constitutional Law I & II, Criminal Procedure, Advanced Criminal Procedure, and the First Amendment at the University of Idaho College of Law.. She has also coached the National Moot Court Competition Boise Team and serves as faculty advisor for the *Idaho Critical Legal Studies Journal*, a student-edited journal. In 2014, Professor Sanders was named Faculty Advisor of the Year by the Idaho Law Review. Professor Sanders's scholarship focuses on felony sentencing reform; civil and criminal jury trial rights; LGBTQ equality; and the First Amendment's speech and religious classes. Her work has appeared in the *Hastings Law Journal, the William and Mary Bill of Rights Journal,* and the *University of Michigan Journal of Law Reform*. Professor Sanders also contributed commentary for an edited collection entitled *Feminist Judgments: Rewritten Opinions of the United States Supreme Court*. The collection was published by the Cambridge University Press in 2016. Professor Sanders is admitted to practice in the state courts of Louisiana, New York, and Washington, as well as various federal district and circuit courts

Rebecca J. Tallent, Ed.D., is an award-winning journalist and public relations specialist with more than 12 years' experience as an energy, environmental and financial journalist, plus an additional 20 years' experience as a public relations specialist, primarily with state government agencies. In addition to her UI teaching, Becky was the ombudsman for the Spokane The Spokesman-Review in 2008 and is a member of the UI American Indian Studies faculty. She is also a member of the Society of Professional Journalists (SPJ) and the Native American Journalists Association (she is of Cherokee heritage). In 2013 she was elected to the national SPJ Board of Directors as a Campus Advisor at Large and serves on the SPJ National Education Committee. She earned her Bachelor of Arts in Journalism (1975) and her Master of Education in Journalism (1977) from the University of Central Oklahoma and her Doctor of Education in Classroom Teaching/Mass Communications from Oklahoma State University in 1995. As part of her continuing education, Becky attended the Poynter Institute for Media Studies in the summer of 2007 to learn more about teaching Diversity Across the Curriculum. In 2007-2008, she held a Diversity Leadership Fellowship with the Society of Professional Journalists.

Robert J. Taylor, J.D., in addition to practicing law through Taylor Law & Mediation, PLLC, in Mountain Home, Idaho, Robert also serves as an engineer officer in the Idaho Army National Guard and in 2017 he was hired as the Idaho Army National Guard's public affairs officer. In 2008, he spent six years as a paralegal specialist for the Idaho Army National Guard. Robert attended the College of Southern Idaho before earning a bachelor's degree from the University of Idaho in public relations, a master's in sports administration from American Military University and a J.D. from the University of Idaho College of Law. Before going to law school, Robert worked as a reporter at the Mountain Home News. He was the assistant adviser for the University of Idaho's student media department while in law school and has won four Idaho Press Club awards for his work as a journalist.

47247407R00142

Made in the USA
Middletown, DE
20 August 2017